SOMETHING IS OUT THERE

A LAYMAN'S VIEW OF THE UNIVERSE

JOHN HEWITT

Published by *Words to World Publishing*
Cover, Typesetting and Design by *Words to World Publishing*

ISBN: 978-1-78798-950-4 (print)
ISBN: 978-1-78798-951-1 (eBook)

British Library Cataloguing-in-Publication Data

A catalogue record for this book is available from the British Library.

Printed and bound in the United Kingdom by BookVault.

10 9 8 7 6 5 4 3
27 26 25 24 23

CONTENTS

For Ash who is 'a pearl of great price'

ACKNOWLEDGEMENTS

Thank you to my wife Ashleigh, who not only got to giggle a lot at my terrible grammar and typos but made my text readable. To Heidi Johnston who edited the text; to Josh, Geoff, and Jim C who took the time to read it and give me genuine feedback. I appreciate you all. To Jim K who got me into this. My prayer is that this will be a help to someone for the glory of God!

Soli Deo Gloria

INTRODUCTION

It has been fifteen years since the rise of 'New Atheism' and, although remnants of its militancy still appear, most atheists I talk to are quick to say, 'I don't believe in God, but not like Dawkins.' Generally, people want to dissociate from that kind of firebrand atheism. But, like the background radiation of the Big Bang, a lasting feeling still hangs in the subconscious, suggesting that science stands in opposition to God. I would like to show that this is simply not the case. I want us to see that rather than opposing God, science is really a response to him. Far from disproving the existence of God, science points straight to Him.

This is a book I never intended to write. When the Covid-19 pandemic hit, lockdown unexpectedly gave me a lot of time to read. As I delved into books on cosmology and biology (and got to know my Amazon delivery man, Kevin!) I found that one person was on my mind. I call him Mr Science and Reason. I got chatting to him several years ago and he told me that he was an atheist, explaining that his atheism was based on 'science and reason'. I think he was a little surprised when I replied that science and reason led me to become a Christian. This book is written for him, and others like him, in the hope that they might move a little closer to opening the door to the God who is not only behind science but is the source of reason itself.

My reading list started with the infamous *The God Delusion* by Richard Dawkins. To be honest, by the time I got about a third of the way through I was a little rattled until I began to realise what Professor Dawkins was doing. The book is genuinely an aggressive, belittling attack on religion. So when I genuinely started analysing the content, rather than following the agenda, I thought it was a weak attempt at dismissing God. Thinking through the arguments, and especially looking up Dawkins's references when he is talking out of his field, was eye-opening. Rhetoric is a powerful weapon, and it can cloud shaky arguments. While Dawkins may make some points that are worth considering, the claims he makes go far beyond his basis for making them.

This book is also for people who have been badgered out of belief in God by taunts of stupidity and accusations of backwardness. My hope is that for someone who is doubting, it might in some sense be an arm around the shoulder to steady them. Dawkins himself said that a case for a deist god could be made, and I want to show you that, in this statement, he is right. From the evidence in our natural world, a case can be made that points to a God.

In this book we are thinking simply about our 'origins', and so I should technically confine myself to talking about deism.[1] But Christianity is not deism, in fact, it is very far from it. Christianity makes a case for belief from many areas of study; from cosmology, mathematics and physics, from biology, palaeontology and archaeology, from philosophy, history, intuition and chiefly in revelation. It is a collective argument. I will make several applications, especially in the last chapter, that will bring us straight to Christianity and not leave us where I should, in deism.

[1]   This is the belief that there is something out there, a mind or a being. But that being whatever or whoever it is does not intervene or has no notion of intervening with us.

INTRODUCTION

Since we are only thinking about *origins* in this book, I should tell you where my other two main areas of evidence are coming from. There are two more steps that take you to Christianity. Firstly, there is *intuition*. The things we instinctively know: morality, uniqueness of what a human is, language, beauty, meaning, love etc. all give natural pointers to someone beyond. Secondly, there is *revelation* which is found chiefly in the Bible and the historicity of Jesus Christ.[2] My conviction that there is a God is not because of one strain of evidence, but because of the cumulative evidence that points to Him. Origins will bring you to deism, intuition will bring you to theism, and revelation will bring you to Christianity.

There have been many excellent and convincing responses to the New Atheism movement, and it is not my intention to better them. As a layman who is not a scientist by trade, it would be arrogant to even try. Instead, these are the thoughts, discoveries and convictions of an ordinary man who is trying to understand the universe. An average John writing for average Joes and inviting you to explore with me.

In recent years, many experts have sought to help the general public understand their different specialist fields. I am so thankful that they undertook to do so and, as a result of their work, I am convinced that we can understand this universe to a certain level. The universe is amazing, and the more we understand, the more I find myself filled with an almost 'natural' and intuitive awe that I cannot shake. It is fascinating to hear a cosmologist describe how a star is made, or a physicist explain how iron is produced

---

[2] This is based upon St Paul's argument in the first three chapters of Romans: *The Creation of the World*, 1:20; *The Conscience We Have*, 2:12–16; *God's Revelation*, *The Oracles of God*, 3:1–2.

in the core of a star through fusion or to be shown by a biologist the dynamics of DNA. I hope that this book might even entice you to go on and explore the universe for yourself.

Chapter One will begin by defining what it is to believe. I think this is one of the least understood ideas in modern society, with so many people still thinking belief means 'blind faith'. It does not, and hopefully, we will see this. After that, we will look at four great difficulties and questions, four wedges that push science to its limits. Firstly, what started everything off; why is there something rather than nothing? Secondly, why is this universe so finely tuned? Thirdly, what do we make of this privileged planet? And finally, how does life start in a complex cell? Then we will spend a chapter thinking about science itself, showing that science and faith are not opposites. Then, finally, we will look at Christianity's origin story. In most cases, you should never read the last part of the book first. On this occasion, I encourage it. The final chapters are where I want all my readers to get to, engaging with Christianity's origin story and grappling with what it actually says, rather than listening to strangers on YouTube tell you what they think it means.

I have read a lot of the New Atheist, God-bashing material, and yet I am still a convinced Christian. In fact, I am more convinced than ever. There are good reasons to believe. My calendar for today says 'tús matih leath na hoibre', and it means 'a good start is half the work', so here goes.

CHAPTER 1

IS IT STUPID TO BELIEVE IN GOD?

. . . but then I suddenly realised;
there was a gap behind me too.

Sheldon Vanauken

It is silly, backward and outdated to believe in God, isn't it? That is what we are constantly told, but I want you to know from the outset that I don't think it is one bit silly, in fact, I consider it the most rational thing in the world to believe in God. 'How can faith be rational I hear someone say?' or 'How can you believe in something you don't see, you can't empirically test for, and you cannot prove?' These are the kinds of questions that come off the standard liturgy of any debate on belief in God. The root of the trouble seems to be in defining what the word 'faith' or 'belief' means. What do we mean by saying, 'I *believe* in God?' I wonder what you think? What comes to your mind whenever you hear the words 'faith' or 'belief in God'? Before we consider the idea of belief in God, it is important to spend a little time thinking about what *faith* and this word *believe* is, and what it is not.

In my own land, faith and religious belief have become contentious words, seen as the cause of the 'Troubles' and a source of division in our society. For some, faith indeed is seen as backward, outdated, without relevance, and should be relegated to the past. The common negative stereotypes are often reinforced or made worse by those viewed as 'religious nutcases' who appear on TV and radio programmes shouting, complaining and quoting the Bible, yet never showing any love or compassion for people. Tragically, there are also those for whom faith means bad examples: being shouted at, physically assaulted and suffering all kinds of abuse, all the while being told that God loves you. If this is faith no one could blame you for rejecting it.

Many people misunderstand faith by equating it with 'believing in yourself' or 'thinking positively' in order to achieve your goal. Just look at the 'spiritual' aisle of any bookshop to see titles like *The Power of the Subconscious Mind* or *Be the Best You* or even *The Power of Emotions*. You can do it, believe in yourself. Imagine it, work hard, have faith in yourself and it will happen!

For others, as I have said, faith in God is simply irrational. Religious belief is akin to closing your eyes, putting your fingers in your ears, ignoring reason and chanting, 'I *believe, I believe, I believe.*' We have been through the Enlightenment. We have had our scientific revolution. We don't need God. There is a scene towards the end of *Indiana Jones and the Last Crusade* where Harrison Ford comes to a chasm that's impossible to cross. As he prepares to make the 'leap of faith', his father shouts, '*Believe boy, you must believe.*' So, he shuts his eyes, clutches his heart, extends his foot and steps out, landing on a piece of rock that had not been visible from his vantage point. 'That's it,' some would say, 'faith is not needed because the stone was there all along!' We have the rock of science, why do we need this empty, blind, worked-up faith?

I think it is fair to say that whenever the words 'faith' or 'belief' are mentioned, there are many views on what that means. We can't deal with all the issues but I would like to consider the problems with two approaches to faith in particular, before turning to the question of what faith actually is.

'IF IT WORKS FOR YOU'

When you meet someone for the first time, you generally go through some standard questions: *What is your name? Where are you from? What do you do for a living?* I usually answer, *My name is John, I live in Armagh and I teach the Bible for a living.* Cue the tumbleweed blowing across the room. Saying you teach the Bible is like conversational Marmite; people are either really interested or really repelled. I often try to ease the tension by making a bad joke about 'having shares in every coffee shop in town' or saying, 'Don't worry, I have been certified,' (they don't believe me!). This is often followed by the response, *Well if it works for you, that's great.* At this, I usually cringe a little and then the conversation moves on.

This response is telling in terms of where we are in our thinking as a society. We place more emphasis on personal experience than we do on actual truth. I recently watched a video of a man interviewing people on a university campus, on the subject of identity. The interviewer, who is white, starts off by saying, 'What if I said to you I was of Asian origin? What would you say?' They respond, 'Good for you!' Similarly, they affirm his statements as he goes on to make increasingly ridiculous claims about his gender, ethnicity, height and more. In our culture, we place so much value on tolerance that we willingly embrace it at the expense of truth.

So, if someone believes that the tree in their garden is an extension of God, and every morning they bow down to it, we affirm, 'That's great if it works for you!' What? Really? Is that not (dare I say it) 'silly'? Would it not be the better and more loving thing to ask a few questions to find out how the person came to this view and assess their sanity? Or, would that be deemed 'judgemental'?

I believe in freedom of speech and belief but does that mean we can't believe in the idea of 'the truth'? And if there is a God, would He not be scratching his celestial head at the prospect of our tree worshipper?

To believe when there is no basis for it is absurd and the Bible's response to that kind of belief is 'pity'.[3] Writing about the resurrection of Jesus, the apostle Paul declares, 'If there is no resurrection, our faith is futile . . . we are of most men to be pitied.'[4] Why believe it, practise it or teach it if it is not? It only has real value if it is true. If our tree worshipper is going through a crisis and prays to the tree, what will happen? What can that tree do for them? Nothing!

You might argue that you feel good when you rub a crystal, chant to the forest or meditate. I have experienced the spiritual world and I don't doubt the feeling or the experience, but is 'feeling something' enough? Is that our rule of thumb: 'I feel good' or 'I have experienced this so it must be good'? What if I feel good when I steal something? If my experience causes me to have an affair, does that make it OK? Should we not be making decisions based on what is true, rather than simply on what feels good? And, if we believe that there is a spiritual world out there, both

---

[3]   1 Corinthians 15:9
[4]   1 Corinthians 15:17

good and bad, would it not be dangerous to freely open ourselves up to all of it without testing what is good or bad, regardless of the feeling or experience?

What are the foundations for what you believe? Why do you believe what you believe? If what you believe is based purely on what you 'feel to be true' or what you have experienced, have you ever been wrong? Do we not need to base our faith on truth?

If this is true, the approach to faith that says, 'Well, if it works for you,' doesn't get us very far. Faith, if it is to be of any use at all, will have to be based on what is factual and what is actual! For Paul, the evidence for the resurrection—from the Old Testament, eyewitnesses, the lives of Jesus' followers, the empty tomb and then also from personal experience—was overwhelming. He believed it because it was true and he asks us to do the same. Biblical, evidential faith is based not on what a person *decides* is true, but on what *is* true. The faith at the heart of Christianity not only stands up to scrutiny but it is factually based in history—it makes sense of our intuition and it works in our lives.

FAITH, SCIENCE AND REASON

In the introduction, I mentioned my atheist friend, Mr Science and Reason. While he claimed that science and reason led him away from God, I explained how I came to believe that we were created and that, if we are created by and for a personal God, then the most reasonable and sensible thing was to live for Him.

So how do he and I, both reasonably intelligent men looking at the same world, come to such opposite views? This paradox is not just true of ordinary men like us, but also of many who are experts in their fields. What are we to say to world-renowned scientists like Francis Collins (the former head of the Human Genome Project and a convinced Christian) and Richard Dawkins (an evolutionary biologist and probably the world's most famous atheist)? Both scientists, both looking at the same material, but coming to opposite conclusions. Or John Lennox (Professor of Mathematics at the University of Oxford), a convinced Christian, and Lawrence Krauss (Professor at Arizona State University) who is an atheist. Or take the late Christopher Hitchens, (former contributing editor of *Vanity Fair*) who was an atheist and C. S. Lewis (writer and Professor of English at Oxford University) who was a convinced Christian. How do these people in similar disciplines with similar minds come to such different conclusions?

In our experience of life, we are not completely ruled by reason. Far from it![5] We all come from different backgrounds: some difficult, some nurturing. We have different systems of belief: some 'god'-based, some not. We have different moral values: some liberal some conservative. And, whether we realise it or not, we are all biased. How could we not be influenced by the things that have shaped us? It is sometimes said that people become Christians because of what faith offers them: life after death in heaven, the hope of reunion with loved ones who have died, forgiveness of sins, freedom from guilt, etc. Because they have an emotional need, they choose to believe it. It is 'opium for the masses'. For many, what Christianity offers is appealing. But, for some, what atheism offers is also appealing: no moral constraint, freedom to do what you want with no 'cosmic Big Brother' watching over your shoulder. Thomas Nagel, New York University philosopher, said:

---

[5]   See C. S. Lewis, *Mere Christianity*, 1942, Chapter 11: *Faith*, pp. 138–143

I want atheism to be true and am made uneasy by the fact that some of the most intelligent and well-informed people I know are religious believers. It isn't just that I don't believe in God and, naturally I hope that I am right in my belief. It's that I hope there is no God. I don't want the universe to be like that![6]

Aldous Huxley, the great writer and philosopher, said:

I had bad motives for not wanting the world to have meaning . . . for myself, as no doubt for most of my friends, the philosophy of meaninglessness was an instrument of liberation from a certain system of morality. We objected to the morality because it interfered with our sexual freedom.[7]

My point is this: we all have biases. That cannot be denied. But no matter what our bias is, we must try as much as possible to be objective in our search for what is true.

Take my friend whose rejection of God was based on 'science and reason'. Did you notice his approach of putting faith and reason in opposite corners, it is one or the other? This highlights a second problem that lies in how you define faith. In his mind, belief in God is the height of intellectual suicide. His idea of faith means, 'leaving your brain at the door'. Why? Because 'believing' in something requires one hundred percent proof. 'Prove your God exists and I will believe,' he says. I think this is a mistake on two levels.

[6]   Thomas Nagel, *The Last Word*, 1997, pp. 130–1
[7]   Aldous Huxley, *Ends and Means*, 1937, quoted in a sermon by D. A. Carson *'Faith and Doubt'*

First, it is a *category mistake*. To ask for proof of God is to misunderstand God. He is not part of this cosmos but stands outside of it. He is the creator of it and so He is separate from it. He is transcendent, meaning He stands apart from this world. To ask for proof of God like you would ask for proof that there are koala bears in Australia is to ask a very naïve thing according to most of the philosophical world. Because koala bears are part of this world you could investigate and find them, and if you wanted proof, you would do so. But what experiment could you set up to find God? You can't! It is an impossible ask! If He is outside of our world, it is naïve to ask someone to prove He exists before you believe.

Second, it is an *actual mistake*. What I mean by this is that it does not work in actual life. In reality, we don't always live our lives according to proof. Senior Fellow at the Discovery Institute in Seattle, David Berlinski, says, 'We can make no sense either of daily life or the physical sciences in terms of things that are seen.'[8] You see, we believe things in everyday life, quite naturally, that we cannot prove. For example, think about law decisions in the courts. Can you prove without doubt that all who testify are telling the truth, or that the judge or jury is without prejudice? Can you even trust your friends, one hundred percent? Can you prove beauty in art or music? While we cannot prove them, we believe in justice, love, friendship and beauty. I cannot prove my wife loves me but I believe it. I cannot prove that when I leave something in a shop to be printed the job will be done but I believe it will. I cannot prove that a sunset over Armagh City is beautiful but I believe it is. Is that belief blind or without warrant? Is there

---

[8]   *The Devil's Delusion*, David Berlinski, 2009, p. 45

no evidence for it? No, I believe my wife loves me because I hear what she says and see what she does for me. The reputation of the printers is excellent. The sunset over the lake fills me with awe. I believe, not because there is no evidence, but because the things I have witnessed, experienced, heard and seen all point to the same conclusion. I cannot prove it, but I am fully convinced by the evidence and I believe it.

The reality is that everyone lives by faith, even those with a secular worldview.[9] Charles Taylor says, 'Secularism is a new set of beliefs, not an absence of belief.' He gives two reasons. First, an atheist lives by faith because they cannot prove God doesn't exist. When they live as though there is no God they are living by faith, according to their belief. They are betting their life that there is no God! Again, what experiment or scientific test could you use to prove that all matter came into existence by itself? Second, every secular person lives by two main values. Firstly, equal human rights: the belief that every human is equal in value and dignity. Secondly, universal benevolence: the belief that I should be concerned about the poor and the needy not just in my local community but everywhere. Is it possible to prove scientifically that all humans are equal? We can't. These are matters of faith! Do you see that 'Secularism is a new set of beliefs, not an absence of belief'?

If this is true then it follows that no one has the higher moral ground. A Christian can't say, 'I am just following the evidence but those atheists are just shutting their eyes to the facts.' Neither can an atheist say, 'I'm rational, Christians are irrational.' Both

---

[9]   Based on *Making Sense of God*, 2006, Tim Keller, Chapter 2: *Isn't Religion Based on Faith and Secularism Based on Science?*

positions, Christian and atheist, are a set of beliefs, not a set of proofs! In a debate with Michael Shermer, John Lennox made the point that moral living is not based on proof. Dismissing it as nonsense, Shermer replied, 'It is not faith to believe in morals.' To which John Lennox responded, 'Why, don't you believe it?'

Human value makes sense if you believe there is a moral God who made humans in His image, giving them dignity and imprinting them with a sense of his moral likeness. It doesn't make sense in a world where evolution teaches that the strong eat the weak and that the weak are weeded out rather than helped or cared for. So, universal benevolence makes sense in a world with God but it is a massive leap of faith for an atheist! As one man put it, 'Man descended along with apes by the process of the strong eating the weak, therefore love one another!'

FAITH AS THE BIBLE DESCRIBES IT

If there is a God and He has created us, He created our minds and He wants us to use them. Jesus constantly appeals to the minds of people—the word 'teach' (or taught / teaching) appears repeatedly in the Gospels. Even in Mark's Gospel—which is generally considered a more action-based eyewitness document—it is the most repeated word! Why did Jesus teach? Because He wanted people to think and to be convinced that He is who he says He is. The first commandment and the most important thing God wants us to do is to 'Love the LORD God' with all that we are, including 'all our **MINDS**'.[10]

---

[10]   Mark 12:28–34

One of Jesus' disciples, Thomas,[11] had many doubts that Jesus had risen from the dead. As a twin, he knew a little about the duplication of bodies, so he made sure to get the right one. What did Jesus do for him? He gave him evidence. He was able to see Jesus, hear him, touch His wounds, smell Him and watch Him eat. Not once does he tell him to shut his eyes, close his ears and 'just believe boy, just believe'. In fact, the opposite is true. Jesus says, 'Open your eyes, listen to my voice; here is the evidence.'

One great example of faith in the Bible is a man called Abraham. Describing Abraham's faith in Romans 4, Paul twice uses the phrase, 'he considered'. That is, he calculated it out, because biblical faith is a 'reasoned trust'.[12] When the apostle John is trying to explain this he talks about trusting people.[13] This is why I think it is difficult for some to believe in God because He is not a concept or a principle but He is a person. Think for a moment; how do you come to trust someone? No one would expect you to switch off your mind, give someone your spare key, lend them your bank card and welcome a person fully into your life. That would be naïve, and faith is not and never should be naïve. Instead, it is a weighing up of the evidence, an understanding of character, and an uncovering of truth. That is a considered reasoning.

Having said all this, it is also true that no one will ever come to believe in God because of reason alone. Faith in the Bible is always a response to God. 'Faith comes by hearing and hearing by the words of Christ,' says Paul.[14] God speaks to them to let them see the truth and people respond to His voice. The Bible

---

[11]   John 20:24–31
[12]   John Stott, *The Bible Speaks Today: The Message of Romans*, 1994
[13]   1 John 5:8
[14]   Romans 10:17

speaks of faith as being 'granted' to people. This does not mean that God overrules and people are coaxed against their will, but rather that God will 'enlighten' the person at certain points in their life, enabling them to come to faith. It's like being in a dark room and someone flicks on the light so you can see things clearly. This is what God can do. He wants people to come to know Him. Maybe you know this by experience or perhaps you are on this journey now and that's why you are reading this. Maybe dots have been connected and you are thinking more about spiritual things. That is God working: showing Himself to you and wanting you to know Him.

So, what is faith? Faith is the gap! In Sheldon Vanauken's book, A *Severe Mercy*, he tells the story of how he met and then lost his wife. It is both brilliant and heartbreaking. As he tells the story he recounts how he came to faith as an atheist who struggled with wanting proof:

> I began to see a gap between the possible and the proved, it would take faith to cross it and I didn't want that. If I was going to stake my whole life on the risen Christ, I didn't want there to be any gap between the possible and proven, I wanted proof, I wanted to be sure. I wanted letters of fire across the sky that Jesus is risen. But then I suddenly realised; there was a gap behind me too. Perhaps the leap to acceptance was a horrifying gamble—but what of the leap to rejection? I couldn't prove that Jesus was God, but I certainly couldn't prove that he was not. This was not to be borne. I realised that I could not reject Jesus without a great step of faith. But then I began to realise that

> I could not go ahead without a great step of faith. There was only one thing to do, once I saw that the gap behind me was every bit as big as the gap before me to Jesus.[15]

That is faith: stepping across the gap. Not like Indiana Jones with his eyes closed, but as Thomas did with all his senses involved in the evidence. Think of the different levels of evidence you have been given and see the gap on both sides, for God or against Him. Only you can make the decision. God will not force you; He will not coerce you, but He will help you to see.

We are going to look at the evidence God has given us, not in the greatest detail but enough to get you started. If you dare, you can ask God to help you and to show you what is true. Then you can decide where the 'gap' is greater: before or behind. And make the choice.

[15]   Sheldon Vanauken, A Severe Mercy, 1977

CHAPTER 2

THE JUST BEFORE—THE FIRST CAUSE

. . . the first question.

Martin Heidegger[16]

Sir Charles Lanyon is one of Ireland's most famous architects, designing buildings such as Belfast Castle, Palm House in the Botanical Gardens, the Crumlin Road Gaol and Queen's University. Although he designed them all, you would never expect to come across him hidden in a wall as you walked down a corridor in Queen's. However, when you explore several of his buildings you start to get a sense of his style of design and the personality of the man himself. The appearance of the windows and the finish on the gable-ends and roof trusses all tell you something about the architect. You do, in a sense, start to see him through his work. C. S. Lewis wrote:

> If there was a controlling power outside the universe, it could not show itself to us as one of the facts inside the

[16] Martin Heidegger, *Introduction to Metaphysics* quoted in William Lane Craig *On Guard*, 2015, p. 33

universe—no more than the architect of a house could actually be a wall or staircase or fireplace in that house.[17]

If God exists, we should not expect to see Him physically within the system.[18] Yuri Gagarin, the first human to go into space, is supposed to have said, 'I don't see any God up here.' Of course, he could have looked for the rest of his life and not seen Him as a physical person in this physical world. Instead, like an architect, we should expect to see hints of His creative personality, His power and ingenuity, giving us clues to His existence in this universe. This is what we are going to look for, the strands of evidence that God has left for us, the clues to His existence, the divine fingerprints on the universe.

As I have tried to understand the arguments within the current popular books on cosmology, biology and philosophy, I have found myself filled with wonder at the scale and intricacy of the universe. At the same time, trying to grasp it has also given me a headache! Given that these areas of study go far beyond my expertise, I don't want to say anything half right or even flat out wrong. So, I am taking guidance from Augustine who said:

> It is a . . . dangerous thing . . . to hear a Christian presuming the meaning of Holy Scripture, talking nonsense on (matters of science): and we should take all means to prevent (it).'[19]

---

[17] C. S. Lewis, *Mere Christianity*, p. 24
[18] If he chooses to enter this system, that is his prerogative.
[19] Augustine, *The Literal Meaning of Genesis* quoted, *Darwin, Creation and the Fall*, 2009, p. 203

To prevent this 'talking nonsense' I will be drawing from and quoting those who are experts in their fields. I will disagree little with their science, but sometimes with their conclusions.

I take heart that there are certain aspects of this universe that give us clues that are accessible and within our grasp. Whether that is a child asking the question, 'Why is there something rather than nothing?' or a world-renowned physicist asking, 'Why is the universe expanding rather than retreating?', both can perceive evidence, both can see the fingerprints of God all around us.

I should say that in talking about 'clues' and 'evidence', you could mistakenly get the impression that it is a cosmic game of 'hotter and colder'. It is not. God wants us to know He is there, He has done all He can to reach us, and He can show us if we let Him. Trusting a person is a very different thing from solving a puzzle. When you follow the evidence for Christianity, you will see that from cosmology to biology, from mathematics to philosophy, from history to intuition and then to revelation itself, there is a cumulative argument that is impressive, ending with Jesus Christ.[20]

THE UNCAUSED CAUSE

Let's start at the beginning, or before the beginning, and ask the question of the child and the physicist: 'How did we get here?' or 'Why is there something rather than nothing?' Martin Heidegger, the great German philosopher said, 'That is the question . . . the first of all questions.' What started everything off? What is the first cause of all causes? Things don't spontaneously appear

---

[20]   This is twenty steps further in the argument.

or happen without a cause; something must have started the whole process.

Cause and effect is an undeniable core principle that runs through the universe. It is a cornerstone of science, and it is part of life. My knees hurt because I went to a boot camp this morning and I am nearly forty—cause and effect! My laptop is on because I hit the 'on' button with my finger—cause and effect! Everything (and I mean *everything*) we know about this universe is dependent on a cause outside of itself. Things fall because of gravity, elements emerge due to dying stars, you were born because of the actions or decisions of your parents, and the tree moves because of the wind. If this core principle runs through this universe, which itself is just a huge pile of such reliant processes, then it follows that even the universe would have to be dependent on some cause outside of itself.[21]

Imagine a set of dominoes all lined up in a row. You hit the first domino, then the first hits the second, then the second hits the third and on it goes. The first cause is your finger, the thing that starts the 'domino rolling' so to speak! It can't be another unaided domino because a domino can't move itself. It needs an outside input. Now, this is the point, if this universe had a beginning it must have a first cause. It must have had something to get it going, something out of the loop, a celestial finger to start the domino rolling. This is what Thomas Aquinas called the 'Uncaused Cause' or 'Unmoved Mover'.

The more we think about it, the more we come to see why this question is asked both by the simple child and the renowned philosopher. This forceful argument is basic and intuitive to us,

[21]   Timothy Keller, *The Reason for God*, 2008, p. 129

and this has been the case down through the centuries[22] from the time of John Philoponus of Alexandria in the 4th century to Al-Ghazali in the 11th century, on to Bonaventure in the 13th and John Locke in the 17th and then Immanuel Kant in the 18th century. It has grown and developed and has recently been coined the 'Kalam Cosmological Argument' by William Lane Craig in the 20th century.[23] As David Berlinski put it, 'Some form of this argument has appeared in every human culture. It is universal.'[24] Put simply, it is an argument that has lasted because it is deeply instinctive to us and formidable in its logic. The argument says, 'Whatever begins to exist has a cause, the universe had a beginning, therefore the universe has a cause.'

. . . A BEGINNING?

For many centuries, the prevalent thinking of Western society was dominated by Greek influence. The Greeks taught that the stuff that made up the universe was eternal and so there was no need for a beginning. In the last one hundred years there has been a massive shift in our understanding as this ancient idea of an eternal universe has lost all credibility in the scientific community. The majority now realise that all the evidence points to our cosmos having an actual starting point. Why the shift in understanding? What has caused such widespread belief that the universe had a beginning?

[22]   For a good account of this history of thought see William Lane Craig: *https://www.reasonablefaith.org/writings/popular-writings/existence-nature-of-god/the-kalam-cosmological-argument* or Lee Strobel, *The Case for a Creator*, Chapter 5: *The Evidence of Cosmology: Beginning with a Bang.*

[23]   Lee Strobel, *The Case for a Creator*, 2004, p. 97–98

[24]   David Berlinski, *The Devil's Delusion*, 2009, p. 63

Firstly, it was the discovery that this universe is expanding. Albert Einstein's breakthrough in discovering the theory of relativity in 1917 was a game changer. It uniquely linked space and time which revolutionised the way we think about the universe. But in doing so, he suspected that the universe was not static, but was moving and so not eternal in that sense. He resisted this idea and fudged his equations placing in his equation a 'cosmological constant', a repulsive force, to make the equation work. This, in his own words, was the greatest mistake of his career because it turned out that this type of force is present. Following this in 1927 George Lemaître, a Belgian priest and physicist, proved Einstein's maths of an expanding universe and in 1930 he further proposed that our expanding universe began as an infinitesimal point, 'the primeval atom . . . a day without a yesterday'![25] On New Year's Day in 1925, Edwin Hubble published the results of a two-year study of 'so-called' spiral nebulae. Using Henrietta Swan Leavitt's work from 1912, where she catalogued the stars and their brightness, Hubble proved that certain Cepheid stars were too distant to be inside the Milky Way and subsequently discovered the Andromeda galaxy. Then, building on Vesto Slipher's work from 1912, he was able to take those findings and make comparisons. This meant that in 1929 he discovered, by analysing the wavelength of the light coming from stars (noticing they were shifting red), that they were all moving away from us. If you have ever had an ambulance fly past you with its siren on, you will understand this. The sound pitch changes as it moves away, or when it comes toward you. This is called the Doppler Effect, and it

---

[25] George Lemaitre: https://beyondthesestonewalls.com/blog/gordon-macrae/a-day-without-yesterday-father-georges-lemaitre-and-the-big-bang

works for light too. Whatever direction he looked, the light shifted red, and he confirmed what had been predicted; that space itself was stretching out. Taking theory and experimentation together, it was clear that our universe was expanding.

Secondly, in 1962 Arno Penzias and Robert Wilson detected by means of a hum in their equipment a signal in the night sky that later turned out to be a remnant of the microwave radiation left over from the origin of the cosmos. Then in the mid-1960s Roger Penrose and Stephen Hawking demonstrated that there was a start to the universe, a 'singularity' as it has been coined. So, the late Stephen Hawking says, 'Almost everyone now believes that the universe, and time itself had a beginning.'[26] So, from Einstein to Hubble we see an expanding universe and from Penzias to Hawking we move back to the singularity, that point of a beginning. We are without doubt about this. There was a commencement to this universe; a starting point where and when everything began to exist.

It is interesting though, that not all the scientific community were in favour of a starting point to the universe. In fact, it was highly resisted. The name 'Big Bang' was coined by the astronomer Sir Fred Hoyle, who used it as a term of derision because he didn't like the idea of a starting point. As Stephen Hawking himself noticed:[27]

---

[26] Stephen Hawking and Robert Penrose, *The Nature of Time and Space*, 1996, p. 20, quoted in Timothy Keller, *The Reason for God*, 2008, p. 128

[27] This is not to criticize science in its natural pursuit or scientists themselves. Fred Hoyle was a brilliant man, responsible for the formulation of stellar nucleosynthesis. But it is to make the point, that, no matter how brilliant the man or woman, there can be bias!

Many scientists were unhappy with the universe having a beginning, because it seemed to imply that physics broke down. One would have to invoke an outside agency, which for convenience, one can call God, to determine how the universe began. They advanced theories in which the universe was expanding at the present time, but didn't have a beginning. One of these was 'the steady state' theory, proposed by Herman Bondi, Thomas Gold, and Fred Hoyle in 1948 . . . Another attempt to avoid the universe having a beginning . . . was by two Russians . . . this result was very convenient for Marxist Leninist dialectical materialism, because it avoided awkward questions about the creation of the universe. It therefore became an article of faith for Soviet scientists.[28]

Notice their effort is driven by an agenda, to keep God out of the issue. The geneticist Richard Lewontin famously remarked in, *The New York Review of Books*:

We take the side of science in spite of the patent absurdity of some of its constructs . . . in spite of its failure to fulfil many of its extravagant promises of health and life, in spite of the tolerance of the scientific community for unsubstantiated just-so stories . . . we cannot allow a Divine foot in the door.

[28]   Stephen Hawking, *Brief Answers, to the Big Questions*, 2018, p. 47–48

David Berlinski comically replies:

> If one is obliged to accept absurdities for fear of a Divine
> Foot, imagine what prodigies of effort would be required
> were the rest of the Divine Torso found wedged at the door
> with some justifiable irritation demanding to be let in.[29]

You can see what he is saying. These are renowned scientists
openly stating that they cannot accept certain scientific findings
because it unsettles their atheistic worldview. If there is partiality
here, I can't help but wonder where else it might be found. Now,
as noted in the last chapter, we all have a bias. The church, not
just the scientific community, has also been guilty of this down
through the years. It happens on both sides. John Lennox says:

> It is rather ironic that in the 16th century some people
> resisted advances in science because they seemed to
> threaten belief in God; whereas in the 20th century scien-
> tific ideas of a beginning have been resisted because they
> threatened to increase the plausibility of belief in God.[30]

Irony indeed, so we need to do our best to follow where the data
leads us.

[29] David Berlinski, *The Devil's Delusion*, 2009, p. 9
[30] John Lennox, *God's Undertaker*, 2009, p. 68

'MUCH ADO ABOUT NOTHING'

So, we have left the early Greek thinking of an eternal universe for the recent discoveries that confirm a beginning to this cosmos. Let's plug this into our hypothesis:

> Whatever begins to exist has a cause, the universe had a beginning, therefore the universe has a cause.

We have seen that whatever begins to exist has a cause and therefore that the universe has a cause. That is clear. Now comes the question, how did it begin? What was this cause? What was it like one second before the initial surge of energy? Something cannot come from nothing, can it? The answer to this depends on how you define nothing. In considering this we need to briefly address two popular books released in recent years: A *Universe from Nothing* by Lawrence Krauss and *The Grand Design* by Stephen Hawking and Leonard Mlodinow.

First, let's listen to Lawrence Krauss explaining why the universe has a repulsive force, the force that earlier we saw Einstein discovered. He says:

> The answer is nothing. By nothing, I do not mean nothing, but rather nothing—in this case, the nothingness we normally call empty space. That is to say, if I take a region of space and get rid of everything within it dust, gas, people, and even the radiation passing through, namely absolutely everything within that region—if the remaining empty space weighs something then that would

correspond to the existence of a cosmological term such
as Einstein invented.[31]

So, what causes the universe to expand? Nothing! (Are you
scratching your head yet?) To be kind, if you replace the word
'nothing' with the word 'particles' (whether virtual or not) you
can perhaps start to understand what Krauss means, but what
he says is 'nothing'. Earlier in his book he rails against the philosopher and theologian defining nothing as 'non-being'.[32] That is,
what everyone else in the world would mean by nothing; namely
nothing. What he really means by 'nothing' is in fact a 'quantum
vacuum', or a 'void' as Guido Tonelli calls it which, as he goes
on to say in the rest of his argument, is made up of particles.[33]
He means that there is something there. Now, he is an eminent
scientist and I do not doubt his science, but do you see what he
is doing? He is redefining nothing. Any sensible person can see
that this is wrong. Defending Krauss's book on the BBC's *Question Time*, Richard Dawkins said, 'The universe can come from
nothing,' to which the man on the panel beside him replied, 'Do
you mean that nothing is nothing?' Dawkins replied, 'Well, it is
not nothing.' The audience burst out laughing and you can see
why. They tried to redefine nothing to say that nothing actually contains something. 'The void that we are speaking about is
not a philosophical concept,' says Tonelli (a little more honestly):

> It is a particular material system, one in which matter
> and energy are null. It is a state of zero energy, but it

[31] Lawrence Krauss, A *Universe from Nothing*, 2012, p. 58
[32] *ibid.* p. xiv
[33] Guido Tonelli, *Genesis, The Story of How Everything Began*, 2019, p. 37

is a physical system like all others that can be investigated, measured and characterised ... It is a living thing, a dynamic and constantly changing substance, full of potential, pregnant with (particle/anti-particle) opposites. It is not nothingness; it is on the contrary a system overflowing with unlimited quantities of matter and antimatter.[34]

The mathematics is elegant and again I am not denying their point, but it is still something, rather than the plain nothing we know about. William Lane Craig, in defining the 'nothing' we are familiar with, refers to Homer's *Odyssey*, when Odysseus introduces himself to the Cyclops as 'No man' or 'Nobody'. One night, Odysseus puts out the Cyclops's eye. His fellow Cyclopes hear him shout 'Nobody is killing me! Nobody is killing me!' You see the problem: *nobody* is not really *nobody*, and in science a *quantum vacuum* is not really a '*nothing*'. To start calling these values 'nothing' is at best a redefinition and at worst an attempt to mislead. Now, in one sense, all they are really doing is adding another domino. Rather than answering the question they are just pushing it back by saying that nothing is actually something. They are not telling us what we really want to know, which is, 'Where did the something, the particles, the void come from?' Their 'nothing' might be an answer to some question, but not to ours.

Secondly then, Stephen Hawking and Leonard Mlodinow, in the conclusion of their book *The Grand Design*, write:

---

[34] *ibid*, p. 39, 41–42

Because there is a law like gravity, the universe can and will create itself out of nothing . . . Spontaneous creation is the reason there is something rather than nothing, why the universe exists, why we exist. It is not necessary to invoke God to light the blue torch paper and to set the universe going.[35]

In redefining terms, they are really doing the same thing here as Lawrence Krauss. But instead of particles making up nothing, they have the law of gravity making up nothing. John Lennox wrote a book in response, in which he says:

Hawking assumes, therefore, that a law of gravity exists . . . the main issue for now, is that gravity or a law of gravity is not nothing, if he is using that word in its usual philosophically correct sense of nonbeing. If he is not, he should have told us . . . When physicists talk about nothing, they often appear to mean a quantum vacuum, which is manifestly not nothing. In fact, Hawking is surely alluding to this when he writes, "We are a product of quantum fluctuations in the very early universe."[36]

Again, all they are doing is putting in another domino. Where did this 'matter' that makes up 'nothing' come from? Where did this law of gravity come from? Can you see it? It doesn't answer the question, it just moves it back one position! Now these are eminent, brilliant men and I don't want to unnecessarily criticize

[35] Stephen Hawking and Leonard Mlodinow, *The Grand Design*, 2010, p. 180
[36] John Lennox, *God and Stephen Hawking*, 2010, p. 30

them but their logic here is off. You cannot get something from nothing; we need a First Cause!

INFINITE TURTLES?

It is here we arrive at a limit of science. If the scientific method studies the material world, here the cosmologist has no space, time or matter to study, and so we have an obvious limit. Enter the philosopher, and we have seen a strong, lasting philosophical argument based on our scientific understanding of how this world works. But we can be wrong. This is where a third level comes in: revelation. God has reached in and given us the Bible. At this point, I can imagine the eyebrows raise a little, and I understand that for the moment, but stay with me. Let's just ask the question, is it true? Does what it says about our origins fit?

We have seen that this universe, which has had a beginning, must then have a cause. It must be something outside our system, or an 'outside agency'[37] that began the process. Could this be God? The astonishing thing is that the kind of being needed to both start and maintain the universe is exactly the person described in the pages of the Bible: a unique being who exists without a cause, who did not spring out of nothing, who exists beyond time, who is His own cause and is the source of everything else. The One who needs no cause in Himself. This description aligns perfectly with the God of the Bible.

Whenever the Greek philosophers were speaking about an eternal universe, the Bible said there was a starting point, that 'In the beginning God created.' Whenever the scientific community

---

[37]   Stephen Hawking, *Brief Answers to the Big Questions*, 2018, p. 47–48

were speaking about a 'steady state universe', the Bible said, 'In the beginning' there was a time when 'God created' and began the whole thing. Whenever other cultures in antiquity were thinking about the start of this cosmos and writing their creation stories,[38] they spoke of their God's coming from the matter of the universe and being inside the loop. The Bible said, 'In the beginning God' who stands outside the loop 'created.' Whenever other civilizations were talking about many gods, deifying the wind and sun and stars etc., for millennia the Bible has said, 'In the beginning God created the heavens,' the sun, moon and stars 'and the Earth'[39] and all the processes involved in the Earth. I think this fact must be taken seriously. In 2003 Dr Andrew Parker, a research leader in the Natural History Museum and professor at Shanghai Jiao Tong University, published a book called *In the Blink of an Eye*, which gives an explanation of the emergence of the eye and the subsequent 'Cambrian Explosion'. He was interested in letters he received from some of his readers telling him to read Genesis 1 and compare his findings. Captivated by the same point I have made, he ended up writing *The Genesis Enigma: Why the Bible is Scientifically Accurate*. He says:

> The Genesis account has no right to be correct. Consider the identity of its writer—when and where he lived; there's no way he could have guessed this thesis as it stands. The very best guess available at the time would have been something very different . . . [40]

[38] Enuma Elish: Babylonian creation myth; Sumerian creation myth; ancient Egyptian creation myths.
[39] Genesis 1:1
[40] Andrew Parker, *The Genesis Enigma*, 2009, p. 15

This is my point; how did these Hebrews, millennia ago, get it so right? How did they know about this one being who existed before any matter existed and created something out of nothing? If this hypothesis was a jigsaw with an exact missing piece, the God of the Bible fits perfectly. Throughout the Bible, God is said to be transcendent,[41] meaning He is outside of time and space, not bound by it, and existing before it. He is uncreated, eternal, powerful, and wise. There seems to be a specific First Cause behind this universe and this God is a fit.

Some struggle, at this point, with this concept. They feel that this is not enough, demanding something behind the One who has created. There is a story about a lecture on the nature of the universe. Part of the way through the talk, a person at the back stands up and denounces the lecturer, claiming that they know how the universe was put together. The Earth, they say, 'Was resting on the back of a giant elephant which stands on the back of a turtle.' The bewildered lecturer responds to his objector by asking, 'What exactly, is the turtle standing on?' 'You may be very clever, young man,' the objector says, 'but you can't fool me. It's turtles all the way down.'[42] I am not saying that there is a giant elephant, supported by an infinite number of turtles, but when I say that God is the person behind this universe, the question often comes back, 'Who is behind God? Who created God?' Then who created that god, and who created that god and who created that god, and on it goes. Infinite turtles.

Just as light must stop somewhere, you cannot have an infinite regress. God, I will again say, is uncreated. But this universe is

---

41   Isaiah 6:1
42   Paul Davies, *The Goldilocks Enigma*, 2007, p. 244

created, it has had a beginning and, as I have been trying to demonstrate, is dependent, or 'contingent', as the philosophers would say. Everything within it shows us this. We are dependent on the sun for energy, on water to live, and on air to breathe; everything within the system is dependent. This infers that the system itself is also dependent. In science, we look at our universe and then made predictions. This is a sound prediction. God is not like this created universe, God is not created, God is 'necessary', and everything stops with Him. He is that First Cause. There are no infinite turtles with God, no infinite regress of god after god after god. God just is.[43] He stands outside of time, space and matter like Sir Charles Lanyon standing outside his building. God is the First Cause behind this universe.

CAUSE MEANS PURPOSE

Again, let me state, 'Whatever begins to exist has a cause, the universe had a beginning, therefore the universe has a cause.' I have said that the best explanation for me is God. Permit me to apply this because, if it is true, it means two immense things. Firstly, this material world is not all there is. If God is transcendent, existing before this universe, then there is another (call it what you will) dimension to this existence and God stands here. This is worth thinking about and has profound implications for our life. Secondly, this world has a purpose behind it and that makes your life significant and valuable. This makes sense.

---

[43] This makes more sense to me. 'Infinite turtles' is not a real argument to be considered, it is the schoolboy question of 'who made God?'. But it can be turned around and asked of the atheist, 'What generated this world?' If you believe that this universe, through chance and necessity, through fluke and blind luck has brought you into existence, then who brought it into existence? It gets us nowhere!

Without sounding arrogant, we know this by intuition. The great stars and quasars out there don't know we exist, but we know they do and that, for all their power and size, we are of more value than them.[44] The reason for this only becomes apparent when you get to know the God behind the universe. Without Him, life is robbed of value and significance.

For my thirtieth birthday, my wife arranged for us to go fly-fishing. This is something I rarely get to do now that life is so busy and so it was a great treat. As I was standing beside the water I thought about the fish in the lake. (I'm assuming there were fish, although I didn't catch many of them!) I began to think about a trout swimming about. Let's call him Trevor. He bumps into another fish, Sammy the Salmon, and they start to chat. Trevor says, 'Sammy, I am sick of it, the water, the darkness, the cold. Sick of it!' Sammy says, 'What are we to do? That's our lot. We are fish!' Trevor says, 'I can do something: I can go up on land!' Sammy protests, 'Trevor, it won't work. It is best you stay down here!' Trevor snaps, 'I am going. I want to kick a football and walk in the breeze.' And so, he goes. He swims over to the water's edge and flops up onto the bank where he begins to suffocate and eventually dies. Why did he die? He died because he was made for the water. That's where he thrived and truly lived. He took measures into his own 'fins' and lived his own life the way he wanted to, rather than the way he was designed to, in the same way that a man driving his sports car off-road is destined to wreck the car because it was not designed to be driven that way. What are we designed for? What is our purpose? If this universe has a cause

---

[44] I owe this thought to David Gooding.

behind it, it means that there is a Cause to live for and the First Cause is our first purpose![45]

If we don't live under God, we destroy the car or we die like Sammy! I meet many people whose bodies are wrecked because of the way they live; their lives have no direction or purpose because they have thrown off belief in a Creator. I repeat, if there is a mind behind the universe, then there is a purpose for your life and that First Cause is our first purpose! People often ask me, 'Why is God relevant in my life?' He is relevant because without Him you are missing out on knowing your significance in this universe. God is the missing piece in the jigsaw of this universe, but He is also the missing piece in the jigsaw of your life. To know Him is to know your First Cause.

[45]   Colossians 1:16; Romans 11:36

CHAPTER 3

JUST AFTER THE START: THE FINE-TUNING

A put-up job.

Fred Hoyle

'Space is big. Really big. You just won't believe how, hugely, mind-bogglingly big it is,' says the start of *The Hitchhiker's Guide to the Galaxy*.[46] Our sun is one among hundreds of billions of stars that make up the Milky Way galaxy, and the Milky Way turns out to be just one among billions of galaxies scattered through space. The gaps between stars are so large they are not measured in miles, but in light years. That is the distance light travels in a year, which is about six trillion miles. Our moon is a 'light second' away, and the sun is eight 'light minutes' away, which gives a little perspective when we say that the Milky Way is an average spiral galaxy 100,000 light years across.[47] With its stars, solar systems, galaxies, clusters of galaxies (our own system has around thirty-four), and super clusters of galaxies, the universe

---

46   Douglas Adams, *The Hitchhiker's Guide to the Galaxy*, 1979
47   Paul Davies, *The Goldilocks Enigma*, 2007, p. 22

is enormous. 'Go out some night into the woods or desert,' says Lawrence Krauss:

> 'where you can see the stars and hold up your hand to the sky, making a tiny circle between your thumb and forefinger about the size of a dime [author's note: a 5p in GBP!]. Hold it up to a dark patch of the sky where there are no visible stars. In the dark patch, with a large enough telescope of the type we now have in service today, you could discern perhaps 100,000 galaxies, each containing billions of stars.[48]

While all this is immense, we now know that it is not a waste. In fact:

> The very hugeness of our universe, which seems at first to signify how unimportant we are in the cosmic scheme, is actually entailed for our existence. This is not to say that there couldn't have been a smaller universe, only that we could not have existed in it. The expanse of cosmic space is not an extravagant superfluity.[49]

This universe, in its grandeur, is necessary for us to exist. If it weren't this big, we would not be here. Our universe seems that it is 'just right'. In recent years, an incredible amount of page space has been given to this 'just right' or as it is known the 'fine-tuning'

---

[48] Lawrence M. Krauss, *A Universe From Nothing*, 2012, p. 21
[49] Martin Rees, *Just Six Numbers*, p. 10

of our universe.[50] Martin Rees in his book *Just Six Numbers* points to six cosmological properties or values that mean:

> Our emergence and survival depend on a very special 'tuning' of the cosmos . . . These six numbers constitute a recipe for a universe. Moreover, the outcome is sensitive to their values: if any one of them were to be 'untuned', there would be no stars and no life.[51]

Physicist Paul Davies tells us that:

> Scientists are slowly waking up to an inconvenient truth, that the universe looks suspiciously like a fix . . . . For 40 years, physicists and cosmologists have been quietly collecting examples of all too convenient coincidences in special features in the underlying laws of the universe that seemed to be necessary in order for life, and hence conscious beings to exist. Change any one of them and the consequences would be lethal.[52]

---

[50] Paul Davies, 1974; Bernard Carr, 1979; Martin Rees, 1979, 2000; John Barrow, 1986; Frank Tipler, 1986; Steven Weinberg, 1989, 1994; Roger Penrose, 1989, 2004; David Deutsch, 1997, 2006; Alan Guth, 1997, 2007; Leonard Susskind, 2005; John Polkinghorne, 2007; Brandon Carter, 2007; Sean Carroll, 2010; Brian Greene, 2011; Stephen Hawking, 2010; Lee Smolin, 2007, 2015. Needless to say, this list of authors includes many of the brightest and most knowledgeable figures in modern physics and cosmology. Although they may disagree with how and why the universe is tuned, they are unanimous in agreeing that the universe is indeed fine-tuned, and that this feature of the universe begs an explanation. See Luke A. Barnes, 2013, 'The fine-tuning of the universe for intelligent life', *Publications of the Astronomical Society of Australia*, 29 (4), 529-564, 2012.

[51] Martin Rees, *Just Six Numbers*, 1999, p. xii

[52] David Berlinski, *The Devil's Delusion*, 2009, p. 110

Imagine that you walk into a room and there is a universe generating machine sitting on the table. On the machine there are thirty-one dials that must be set to one exact spot. If any were off, even to a millionth part—or in some cases a million millionth—there would not be anything; no matter, no galaxies, no stars, no water, no oxygen, no biology, no life. That is precise. Like Baby Bear's porridge, it is 'just right'.

GRAVITY

So, what are these forces? We will start with something that gets us all down, a force that brings us down to Earth with a bang, that keeps our feet on the ground: gravity. If you have ever dropped your phone and shouted in frustration at a cracked screen, or lent too far back on your seat, fallen and had to pick yourself up with a red face, you have succumbed to the grip of gravity. It is probably the one we are most familiar with, the one most intuitive to us, because we see and feel its effects in everyday life.

The discovery of gravity has a rich history. Isaac Newton is most famously joined to gravity and rightly so; in 1687, he wrote his *Principia*, codifying the equations for universal gravity. But no man is an island for his insight was built on Copernicus, Kepler and Galileo's work. These three foundational men made radical discoveries that shaped Newton's thinking. In 1543 Nicolaus Copernicus in the face of Greek wisdom, put the sun at the centre of our solar system, explaining the motions of the planets around us. Between 1609 and 1619 Johann Kepler, based upon the work of Danish astronomer Tycho Brahe, formed three laws of planetary motion. Noticing the shape of the orbit, its speed nearer the sun and then a planet's relation to other planets. This formed a blueprint of how gravity worked among the celestial objects at least. In the late 16th/early 17th centuries Galileo is said to have dropped balls from the Tower of Pisa. What he did, however, was to set up slides to roll balls down to calculate that objects will accelerate at the same rate. For if you drop a weight to the floor from a height of 4ft and the duration of its fall is 0.5 seconds, from 8 ft, it is 0.7 seconds, from 16 ft it is 1 second. Repeat, and you will discover a rule, that the time exactly doubles with every quadrupling of the height.[53] Pretty cool.

Newton's interest was 'how can you have "action at a distance?"'. How can the sun affect the Earth at such a distance? There must be some kind of invisible string or holding force between them. Enter the warm spring day in 1666, twenty-two years before his publication, when Isaac Newton's apple fell from the tree. He started to ponder why things always fall to the ground down here, and why the planets revolve up there. Is this the same force? Newton's genius was that the apple and the heavens are connected. The same force controls both, the planets are just large apples. This force is universal. This was a sweep of genius. He took Kepler's 'descriptions' of the heavenly bodies and offered 'explanations' of why they act the way they do. It has been said that three apples have changed the world: 'Adam's apple, Newton's apple and Steve Jobs' Apple.'[54] I think this is true.

Albert Einstein in the early 20th century thought differently, that it is not a force between objects, as if space is an empty container; but that the gravitational field is space itself, so gravity is what he called 'the curvature of spacetime'. My girls and I play

---

[53] Alan Lightman, *An Accidental Universe*, 2013, p. 106

[54] Marcus Chown, *The Ascent of Gravity*, 2017, p. 4. This was a tweet that appeared on the death of Steve Jobs, the founder of Apple.

a game on our trampoline, where we have a football or two, or a couple of tennis balls. The game is that the balls are not allowed to touch you. But when you stand on the trampoline, they naturally come towards you. Why? Because the trampoline surface is displaced and curved by my mass, so the balls are attracted to us. Matter, in kind of the same way, warps space. So, objects are just following the natural curvature of spacetime. Kepler described it, Newton explained it, but Einstein refined it by showing us what causes gravity. The more mass, the greater it bends spacetime. This is general relativity. Every object with mass attracts every other object with mass, and how strong this is will depend on the distance between them and how big they are. The larger the mass the greater curvature of spacetime and the greater the attraction. This is gravity, and it affects everything.

> [It is the] force [that] grips planets in their orbits and holds the stars together . . . No substance, no kind of particle, not even light itself escapes its grasp . . . it is the organising force of the cosmos.[55]

Gravity is small in strength compared to other forces. A good job it is. If it were a little bit stronger, objects would not be able to grow so big, stars would be smaller and burn out quicker, not giving time for the development of life. It has been mathematically calculated that, in the 'just after' the start of things, the rate of expansion and gravity's attracting force must have differed by less than one part in a million billion. That is 1 in 1,000,000,000,000,000.[56]

---

[55] Martin Rees, *Just Six Numbers*, 1999, p. 27, 35
[56] Antony Latham, *The Naked Emperor*, 2005, p. 4

That's a lot of zeros. My point is that gravity is an exact 'force' in strength itself, and in ratio to other forces to allow this life-giving type of universe to exist. If it was twice as strong, then the sun would be smaller and would shine more than a hundred times as brightly. Its lifetime as a stable star would fall from ten billion to less than one hundred million years, which is probably too short for life to emerge.

Interestingly, gravity only attracts, it doesn't repel. It is not self-limiting like electric charges, having a positive and negative that can attract and cancel itself out. So, the more matter there is in one place, the more it drags in additional material and the stronger the combined gravitational force becomes. It is therefore 'self-amplifying', so that despite its extreme weakness it can add up to become dominant, as happens when stars collapse,'[57] which as we will see we need. Can you see that gravity perfectly works to make life possible?

THE COSMIC GLUE: STRONG NUCLEAR BOND

I am at the stage in life when my daughters' Lego bricks mean walking barefoot around the house at night can be perilous. When they are not causing injuries to my feet, the Lego bricks connect to build a wide range of objects from people to helicopters and more. In a similar way, the universe is made up of little building blocks. Everything physical, from the chair we sit on, to the water we drink to our bodies themselves, is made of cells. Cells are made of molecules. Molecules are made of atoms, Atoms are

---

[57] Paul Davies, *The Goldilocks Enigma*, 2007, p. 164

made of protons, neutrons, and electrons. And so on, to quarks etc. It's like an atomic Lego set containing different pieces from the periodic table, that can make everything from people to helicopters and more.

For life to exist and thrive, we need water, which is simply two hydrogen atoms and one oxygen bonded together. But where do we get the hydrogen or oxygen from? How does any chemistry form? The answer is that they are forged in stars. This was suggested by Arthur Eddington in the 1920s and proved by Fred Hoyle in the 1950s. This process requires high temperatures (a billion degrees) and huge pressure at the centre of stars. The denser the star, the quicker and brighter it burns and the more elements it can make further up the periodic table. These elements, formed in the star's core, are hurled out into space through giant supernova explosions and exist in nature in all the different varieties represented in the 'periodic table'. These are the elements that form our planet and us. In a sense we are 'literally the ashes of long dead stars.'[58] 'We're stardust—or less romantically—nuclear waste.'[59] The place of each atom in the table depends on the number of protons in its nucleus. But how are they held together? Physicists tell us there is a strong nuclear force that binds the neutrons and protons[60] together at the centre of the atom. This is held in exact balance with the electromagnetic and weak atomic force. What would change if it were different? If this strong nuclear force was weaker, then elements further

---

[58] Martin Rees, *Our Cosmic Habitat*, 2017
[59] Martin Rees, *Just Six Numbers*, 1999, p. 52
[60] This is understood at the deeper level with subnuclear particles like 'quarks' and 'gluons'. I will spare both our synapses. For a helpful guide see Max Tagmark, *Our Mathematical Universe*, Chapter 7; Paul Davies, *Demon in the Machine*, Chapter 5; Lawrence Krauss, *The Greatest Story Ever Told—So Far*, Chapter 15

up the periodical table could not properly form. We would have a simple universe composed of hydrogen. If it was stronger, no hydrogen would have survived the original beginning, meaning there would be no fuel for the stars. In any universe with complex chemistry, this strong nuclear force is required to be in the range of 0.006–0.008. This is very precise and very finely tuned. As Paul Davies said in the forward of Hoyle's biography:

> His 1950s epiphany, in which he discovered that the existence of carbon the lifegiving element—hinged sensitively on certain precise details of nuclear physics, gave him a deep sense that the universe was, in his words, 'a put-up job'. For Hoyle, 'the hand of intelligence had left clear fingerprints all over physics on cosmology. It was an unconventional quasi-religious philosophy that rested uneasily with his earlier and vehement anti-God stance.'[61]

This discovery of how fine-tuned this force was, moved this atheistic mindset, to raise an eyebrow and wonder maybe 'something is out there'. This is the power of this argument when we get a hold of it.

THE INVISIBLE MAN: COSMOLOGICAL CONSTANT

In *The Invisible Man*, H. G. Wells depicts the sense of shock that occurs when things appear to move by themselves. Imagine this happening on the cosmic level. We have been thinking about the

---

[61] Simon Mitton, *Fred Hoyle—A Life in Science*, 2005, p. xi

visible macro universe, with its galaxies and stars and planets. Then we thought about the micro world with its nuclear Lego. As humans, in terms of size, we sit just about in the middle, between the macro and micro, which interestingly makes the discovery of these two realms possible. It turns out that all the galaxies, stars, planets, people and elements we can detect, from macro to micro, only account for just under 5% of the entire universe. Enter the invisible man.

In 1933, Fritz Zwicky, a Swiss astrophysicist, argued that the galaxies in clusters should fly apart, and that gravity was not enough to keep them. He thought there must be some 'other' force. Vera Rubin and Kent Ford in the 1960s and 70s studied spiral galaxies. They noticed that the outermost material orbited at the same speed as the innermost, even distant hydrogen orbiting far out beyond the limit of visible stars.[62] This should not have been the case. Everything seemed to be behaving as if there were a greater amount of matter that we cannot see, so she concluded that the spiral galaxy must have been immersed in a gigantic shroud of completely unknown matter.[63] It seemed some mysterious pressure in the vacuum of space was acting in opposition to the force of gravity. This has been called dark energy, or dark matter, or Einstein's 'cosmological constant', which is 'a kind of a vacuum energy which is positive and tends to push everything outwards.'[64]

It seems that the stuff we think is empty space actually acts as a force. This dark energy doesn't emit, reflect, or absorb light; we cannot see it. No one really knows, but it is there. This force

[62]   Martin Rees, *Our Cosmic Habitat*, 2017 p. 71
[63]   Guido Tonelli, *Genesis: The Story of How Everything Began*, 2019, p. 119
[64]   *ibid*. p. 21

is the ultimate 'eminence grise', the supreme 'invisible' elephant or man in the room,[65] not only is it invisible but it hides out in empty space. This energy is what keeps galaxies spiralling and causes the expansion of the universe to accelerate in opposition to gravity. Matter alone cannot do this. If there was only matter in the universe, the expansion would slow down under gravity's influence. It takes a further pressure, that increases rather than decreases.

This sounds mad but it appears to work mathematically, reconciling the measured 'geometry' of space with the total amount of matter in the universe. It turns out that 68% of the universe is dark energy, 27% dark matter and that the remaining 'observable matter' constitutes less than 5% of our universe.

Whatever this strange energy is, as a force in the universe, it is inconceivably precise. Although it is the weakest force in nature, when you put this force next to gravity, you see a unique balance. In a sense, our cosmic history has been a gravitational tug of war between dark matter, trying to push things apart, and gravity, trying to pull things together. If dark energy was a larger force, then the result would have been a stillborn universe, remaining forever dark and lifeless, containing nothing more complex or interesting than nearly uniform gas. If dark energy was a lesser force, the universe would have stopped expanding before any life had time to emerge. All this means that if you want to 'tune the knob' of dark energy to produce complex life-giving galaxies, it must be correct to over 120 decimal places.[66] That is:

---

[65]   Alan Lightman, *The Accidental Universe*, 2013, p. 15
[66]   Max Tagmart, *Our Mathematical Universe*, 2012, p. 141

1,   000, 000, 000, 000, 000, 000, 000, 000, 000, 000,
     000, 000, 000, 000, 000, 000, 000, 000, 000, 000,
     000, 000, 000, 000, 000, 000, 000, 000, 000, 000,
     000, 000, 000, 000, 000, 000, 000, 000, 000, 000.

Out by any margin and it spells doom. Paul Davies says:

> The cliché that "life is balanced on a knife edge" is a
> staggering understatement in this case: no knife in the
> universe could have an edge that thin . . . one is more likely
> to get 400 heads in a row flipping a coin.[67]

Almost impossible.

I have just looked at three knobs on the universe building machine, gravity, the strong nuclear force in binding atoms, and the cosmological constant. Already you start to see the zeros piling up and perceive something of the fine-tuning of this cosmos. There are many others: the rate of entropy, the speed of light, the weak nuclear force, the reality of three-dimensional space, the flatness of our universe, the mass of the various subatomic particles, and the laws of thermodynamics. In fact, according to a 2005 paper by Max Tegmark (MIT), Anthony Aguirre (UCSC), Martin J Rees (Cambridge) and Frank Wilczek (MIT), there are thirty-one[68] of these constants and laws, built into this universe. If any are changed or altered, it makes our universe radically different and, overall, uninhabitable. Nobel Prize-winning physicist, Roger

---

[67]   Paul Davies, *The Goldilocks Enigma*, 2007, p. 170
[68]   Paul Davies says, 'The standard model of particle physics has about twenty undetermined parameters, while cosmology has about ten. All told, there are over thirty "knobs",' (*The Goldilocks Enigma*, 2007, p. 166).

Penrose,[69] has calculated the odds of this happening by chance to be one in $10^{10 \times 123}$. That's a ridiculously large number, greater than the number of atoms in the observable universe! I am not a betting man, but I don't like those odds. This fine-tuning argument, together with the other levels of evidence for believing in a God, has real force. Anthony Flew, a noted atheist who converted to theism in later life said:

> Although I was once sharply critical of the argument of design, I have since come to see that, when correctly formulated, this argument constitutes a persuasive case for the existence of God.[70]

As you can imagine, not everyone comes to this deduction. Again, while not many will argue with the science, some will argue with the conclusion. A recent book, A *Fortunate Universe*, written by Geraint Lewis (an atheist) and Luke Barnes (a Christian), both from Sydney University, offers a brilliant last chapter. In it they discuss their conclusions to the fine-tuned universe. The three options in layman's terms are 'it is what it is', 'the multiverse' or 'the G-word'.[71]

'IT IS WHAT IT IS'

The first option is to say 'it is what it is'. It is futile to ask why it is fine-tuned, because if it wasn't, we wouldn't be here to question

69 Roger Penrose, *The Emperor's New Mind*, 1989, pp. 341–344
70 Anthony Flew, 2007, quoted in Peter S. Williams, *A Sceptic's Guide to Atheism*, 2013, p. 191
71 Geraint F. Lewis and Luke A. Barnes, *A Fortunate Universe*, 2016, p. 323

it. So, if you were playing roulette and you bet on the seven red, and it came up, it is no good asking yourself, 'Why did it come up seven red?' It just did. Like Lady Gaga singing 'Born this Way',[72] it is what it is, why question it? This so-called 'weak anthropic principle' seems quite defeatist to me. It is like a parent shutting down a child's questions by saying 'it just is' or 'why not?'. To say 'it is what it is' is to state the obvious that if the universe was not fit for life, then we would not be here. This circular reasoning does nothing to explain the surprising existence of a life-friendly universe.[73] What if the roulette wheel kept coming up red sevens, thirty-one times in a row? No one would just say 'it is what it is'. This kind of thinking ignores the astonishing nature of these fine-tuned forces. Richard Swinburn, in a slightly sinister analogy, puts it like this:

> Suppose that a madman kidnapped a victim and shuts him in a room with the card shuffling machine. The machine shuffles ten decks of cards simultaneously and then draws a card from each deck and exhibits spontaneously ten cards. The kidnapper tells the victim that he will shortly set the machine to work and it will exhibit its first draw, but unless that draw consists of an ace of hearts from each deck, the machine will simultaneously set off an explosion which will kill the victim, in consequence of which he will not see which cards the machine drew. The machine is then set to work, and to the amazement and relief of the victim the machine exhibits an ace of hearts drawn from

---

[72] ibid. p. 292
[73] Peter S. Williams, A Sceptic's Guide to Atheism, 2013, p. 192

each deck. The victim thinks that this is an extraordinary fact that needs an explanation in terms of the machine having been rigged in some way. But the kidnapper, who now reappears, casts doubt on the suggestion. "It is hardly surprising," he says, "that the machine draws only aces of hearts. You could not possibly see anything else. For you would not be here to see anything at all, if any other cards had been drawn." But of course, the victim is right and the kidnapper is wrong, the fact that this particular order is a necessary condition of the draw being perceived at all makes what is perceived no less extraordinary and in need of explanation. The design's starting point is not that we perceive order, but that order is there. Maybe only if order is there can we know what is there, but that makes what is there, no less extraordinary and in need of explanation.[74]

The fact that there is an event doesn't explain the event itself. To say 'it is what it is' may be true, but it offers nothing to explain 'how it is'! We should be saying, 'Wow, it is!' The fine-tuning of the universe is nothing short of miraculous. Max Tegmart says:

So what are we to make of this fine tuning? First of all, why can't we just dismiss it as a bunch of fluke coincidences? Because the scientific method doesn't tolerate unexplained coincidences.'[75]

[74] Richard Swinburn, Is There a God?, 1996, p. 57–8
[75] Max Tegmark, Our Mathematical Universe, 2012, p. 142

He goes so far as to say that, if we ignore this, we are not being fair to science itself. It demands a response, an answer, an explanation. Francis Collins, the former head of the human genome project that mapped out humanity's genetic code, says, 'The chance that all of these constants would take on the values necessary to result in a stable universe capable of sustaining complex life forms is almost infinitesimal.'[76] It looks like he is right.

THE MULTIVERSE

Is the fine-tuning of this cosmos an incredibly precise thing, or is it just the inevitable outcome of millions of universes being created? An accidental universe[77] among many? Surely if you make enough, one of them is bound to be exact. One of them is bound to pop out eligible for life. This view is called the multiverse, or mega-verse, or even 'the landscape' as coined by Leonard Susskind. This is the 'opinion' not only of Marvel and DC Comics but of such renowned people as Sir Martin Rees, Stephen Hawking and Max Tegmark. They argue for a spontaneous birthing of many universes all existing together in the same field great distances apart or in different dimensions. It is sort of like a cosmic bubble bath with each bubble being a new universe. Many cosmologists and physicists have said this view is on thin scientific ice. Sean Carroll says:

> In modern cosmology, the multiverse is not a theory at all. Rather, it is a prediction made by other theories—theories

---

[76] Francis Collins, *The Language of God*, 2007, *Pocket Books*, p. 74
[77] Alan Lightman, *The Accidental Universe*, 2013, p. 7

that were invented for completely different purposes . . . Two theories, in particular move us to contemplate the multiverse: string theory and inflation . . . both inflation and string theory are, at present, entirely speculative ideas; we have no direct empirical evidence that they are correct. But as far as we can tell, they are reasonable and promising ideas. Future observations and theoretical development will, we hope, help us decide once and for all.[78]

I am not against the idea of a multiverse, I am a bit of a sci-fi geek, but it seems that for the moment this is quite unprovable. As MIT professor Alan Lightman writes:

We must believe in the existence of many other universes. But we have no conceivable way of observing these other universes and cannot prove their existence. Thus, to explain what we see in the world and in our mental deductions, we must believe in what we cannot prove.[79]

David Berlinski further says:

The landscape has, after all, been brought into existence by assumption. It cannot be observed. It embodies an article of faith, and like so much that is a matter of faith, the landscape is vulnerable to the sadness of doubt . . . that

---

[78] Sean Carroll, *The Big Picture on the Origins of Life, Meaning and the Universe Itself,* 2020, p. 307–309

[79] Alan P. Lightman, MIT Professor in *Harper's Magazine: https://harpers.org/archive/2011/12/the-accidental-universe/*

> were physicists to stop writing about the place, the land-
> scape, like Atlantis, would stop existing—just like that.[80]

I find this surprising, in my judgement, it takes more faith than believing in God.

It is not inflation, string theory or the multiverse that bothers me. After all, the Bible talks about 'miracles' and at least one world other than our own; plus, there are Christians who hold to the multiverse. What does trouble me is the scientific community's pursuit of the multiverse on somewhat 'faith-based philosophical' reasons rather than science alone. Paul Davies in his book, *The Goldilocks Enigma*, talks about the unhappiness of the scientific community when papers about the fine-tuned universe began to emerge. Until, that is, the multiverse theory appeared. He says:

> At this stage, atheists began to take an interest. Unhappy
> that the fine tuning of the laws of physics smacked of
> some divine design, they seized on the multiverse theory
> as a neat explanation for the uncanny bio-friendliness of
> the universe.[81]

I find it a little unnerving that the scientific community did not embrace the fine-tuning of this cosmos until they had the multiverse as a 'get-out clause'. Writing with what I think is characteristic honesty, Leonard Susskind says:

[80] David Berlinski, *The Devil's Delusion*, 2009, p. 128
[81] Paul Davies, *The Goldilocks Enigma*, 2007, p. xi

If, for some unforeseen reason, the landscape turns out to be inconsistent—maybe for mathematical reasons, or because it disagrees with observation—I am pretty sure that physicists will go on searching for natural explanations of the world. But I have to say that if that happens, as things stand now, we will be in a very awkward position. Without any explanation of nature's fine-tunings, we will be hard pressed to answer the intelligent design critics. One might argue that the hope that a mathematically unique solution will emerge is as faith based as intelligent design.[82]

The scientific communities motives aside, it is more curious that, if the multiverse is true, the problem of fine-tuning is merely being shifted up a level, from one solitary universe to a multiverse. The question of how these universes got here remains unanswered. What is this complex universe generator and where did it come from?

THE 'G' WORD

It seems that the explanation can be anything under the sun, apart from God. Aliens, multiverse, utter luck, but not God. I cannot help but suspect that science is not the only arbiter to bring some to that 'so-definite' an opinion. Although it really seems to be a fight at times to keep God out. Even the author, astrophysicist and self-described atheist, George Greenstein, has confessed that:

[82]   David Berlinski, *The Devil's Delusion*, 2009, p. 35

The thought instantly arises that some supernatural agency, or rather Agency, must be involved. Is it possible that, suddenly, without intending to, we have stumbled upon scientific proof for the existence of a supreme being? Was it a God who providentially stepped in and crafted the cosmos for our benefit?[83]

But then the door is very quickly shut on the divine foot.

In the Bible, often when He is making promises, God repeatedly invites us to look to the stars. When our world falls apart, or we are riddled with anxiety, it is good to know that the one who framed the stars is able to help us, but it is also important to notice that God wanted man to pursue an understanding of this universe. Believing that God is the creator does not mean we shouldn't pursue this, for God does not put a fence around scientific advancement. There is no cosmic sign saying, 'No Further'. On the contrary, God wants us to investigate. In doing so, we should be warned that we start to develop that 'dangerous' sense of awe that comes from observing a world that is organised and tuned.

The last option, then, is that this cosmos has been fine-tuned by a fine tuner; that there is a designer and mind behind it. Contrary to what many believe, a good number of the scientific community would subscribe to this on some level; it makes the most sense to them. It is the view that genuinely takes hold of the evidence and gives the most apparent answer to a Sherlock Holmes or an Ockham. It is close to impossible for all these forces to be so fine-tuned. Hugh Ross says:

[83] *The Symbiotic Universe*, p. 27; quoted Meyer, *The Return of the God Hypothesis*, 2021, p. 145

Cover America with coins in a column reaching to the moon (380,000 kilometres or 236,000 miles away) then do the same for a billion other continents of the same size. Paint one coin red and put it somewhere in one of the billion piles. Blindfold a friend and ask her to pick it out. The odds are about 1 in 10^{40} that she will.[84]

What does this all point to? John Leslie asks us to imagine a man who has been sentenced to death by firing squad. One hundred trained marksmen stand six feet away. As they fire, every one of them, at the same time, sneezes or makes an involuntary twitch that means they all miss. What are the chances of that happening by accident? It's almost impossible! You couldn't prove it wasn't an accident, but it would be much more reasonable to think it was deliberate. Similarly, you could argue that matter could have appeared without a creator, that it could have been a big accident, but surely it is much more reasonable for there to be a creator. To put it another way, isn't it more unreasonable to base your life on the possibility that a one-in-a-trillion-chance happened? I stand with John Polkinghorne when he says, 'theism provides a more satisfying explanation,'[85] or Freeman Dyson, the Eminent British-American mathematician and Princeton Professor, who said:

As we look out into the universe and identify the many accidents of physics and astronomy that have worked together to our benefit, it almost seems as if the universe must in some sense have known we were coming.[86]

[84]   Hugh Ross, *The Creator and the Cosmos*, 1995, p. 117
[85]   Quoted in Stephen Meyer, *Return of the God Hypothesis*, 2021, p. 144
[86]   Freeman Dyson, *Energy in the Universe*, 1971, p. 50

The welcome mat has been laid out, God has left us clues to his existence, and the fine-tuning of this universe is one of them. Charles Townes, who shared the Nobel Prize in Physics said:

> Intelligent design as one sees it from a scientific point of view, seems to be quite real. This is a very special universe: it's remarkable that it came out just this way. If the laws of physics weren't just the way they are, we couldn't be here at all.

Read the books, Google the fine-tuned universe, and look up at the stars. You might start to see why, in my opinion, all the clues point to a fine-tuner.

CHAPTER 4

OUR PRIVILEGED PLANET

In 1968 the BBC showed pictures from the Apollo 8 mission. For the first time, a crew left the Earth's orbit and travelled to the far side of the moon, taking pictures of things that had never been glimpsed by humankind. President Kennedy had determined that a moon landing should happen before the end of the decade, and this was to be the dry run. It was an exciting endeavour. After some initial problems with the camera were overcome, Frank Borman, Jim Lovell and Bill Anders were the first people to be far enough away from the Earth to be able to see the whole planet with the naked eye. It made a deep impression on the crew. Three and a half hours into the flight Jim Lovell spoke his thoughts to NASA, 'Well I can see the entire Earth now out of the centre window . . . .' Then he repeated, 'Beautiful, beautiful.' There is something about looking at and studying the world around us that produces a kind of awe, almost tempting us to break into song with Louis Armstrong, singing, 'What a Wonderful World'. Interestingly, this tends to happen whether you believe in God or not. Even Richard Dawkins, talks about 'a quasi-mystical response to nature and the universe that is common among scientists and rationalists.'[87] The universe is awe-inspiring. When we think seriously about this cosmos, beginning to understand a little about the factors involved in shaping and maintaining an environment that makes complex life possible, it stirs us. Even something as apparently simple and common as soil is amazing. If you have seen the movie *The Martian*, you may have been struck, as I was, by the complexity of soil and the way it is so perfectly balanced for growing things.

Conversely, the universe as a whole is a terrifying, uninhabitable, and immense place. The 2013 film, *Gravity*, gives a sense of the sheer harshness and danger of space, a place where 'no one can hear you scream'.[88] The vast and inhospitable nature of space has led some to see it as a cosmic waste[89] and to suggest there is nothing special about this planet or ourselves. On my shelf sits a photo called *A Pale Blue Dot*. It was taken in 1990, by Voyager 1, as it was approaching the edge of our solar system. The picture is brilliant: a blue/black backdrop with shafts of light coming nearly vertically down through the shot. Within one of those rays is a pale blue dot; Earth, captured from four billion miles away. Carl Sagan wrote a book with the same title, and in it he said:

> Look again at that dot. That's here. That's home. That's us. On it everyone you love, everyone you know, everyone you ever heard of, every human being who ever was, lived out their lives . . . on a mote of dust suspended in

[87] Richard Dawkins, *The God Delusion*, 2006, p. 11

[88] Ridley Scott's *Alien*, 1979,

[89] Contrary to what is constantly said by leading atheists who should know better (read Christopher Hitchens, *God is not Great*, p. 80). Sir Martin Rees points out that the size of this universe is needed; see, *Just Six Numbers*; Also, Hugh Ross, *Why the Universe is the Way it is*, 2008, p. 32–41.

a sunbeam . . . The Earth is a very small stage in a vast cosmic arena . . . Our posturings, our imagined self-importance, the delusion that we have some privileged position in the Universe, are challenged by this point of pale light. Our planet is a lonely speck in the great enveloping cosmic dark. In our obscurity, in all this vastness, there is no hint that help will come from elsewhere to save us from ourselves. The Earth is the only world known so far to harbour life.[90]

This is bleak by anyone's standards. I have cut the quote down for the sake of space, but I encourage you to Google the image and read his quote in full. Much of what he says is right, but I can't agree with his conclusions on the significance of human life. Remember, as Martin Rees told us in the last chapter, the size of space is necessary for a habitable planet and complex life.[91] The more we study the universe and this *pale blue dot* we call home, the more we see beauty and habitability held in tension with danger and vastness. It is astounding that we have a planet, a solar system, and a galaxy tuned precisely for life.

Carl Sagan again wrote a fiction called *Contact* which was later turned into a Hollywood blockbuster, making the Search for Extraterrestrial Life (the SETI project) a household name. This endeavour sought to beam radio signals out into the universe in the hope that they will be answered by intelligent life. This same spirit of exploration is continued today in the real world by NASA's Exoplanet Science Institute, which is not only searching

[90]   Carl Sagan, *Pale Blue Dot*, 1994, p. 7 ff.
[91]   Martin Rees, *Just Six Numbers*, 1999, p. 10

for planets like our own, but also for complex life. In fact, in recent years there has been a furious hunt for life 'out there', to find exoplanets,[92] that can support complex life. This is done by detecting the small wobble in a star's motion, induced by the gravity in the orbiting planet, and then detecting the dip in a star's brightness when a planet transits across it.[93]

Complex life is a very difficult thing to generate. For that to be possible, precise quantities of certain things must occur, enabling life to thrive and develop. The more we examine our surroundings on Earth, the more the list of features needed is increasing. The factors involved in the original Drake equation (which calculates the likely number of Earth-like planets in the Milky Way galaxy) are expanding. As we will see, we have a planet the right size and the right chemical composition,[94] the right type of sun and the right distance from it, a molten core and suitable atmosphere with a relatively low asteroid and comet impact . . . and so the list goes on. The more we study our surroundings the more we see that we are living on a privileged planet. As Richard Attenborough said, 'It is the only place we have, the only place where life exists as far as we can tell, it is uniquely precious.'[95]

It is not my intention to turn this into a high school science class. Having said that, I'd like to consider a few things about our existence that make life possible, taking a journey from the cosmic galaxy to the very ground under our feet. If this gets tedious, skip to 'Chapter 4: What Shall We Say To These Things?' and you will get a summary of all that will be said in the 'classroom'.

---

[92] You can keep an eye on the search at *https://nexsci.caltech.edu*
[93] Martin Rees, *Our Cosmic Habitat*, 2017, p. xii
[94] Peter Ward, Donald Brownlee, *Rare Earth*, 2004, p. xxiv
[95] David Attenborough, *A Life on our Planet*, p. 43

THE MILKY WAY

In 2003, Hubble's advanced camera sent back a stunning look into the depth of the cosmos. It was taken of a particularly dark part of the sky, about the size of a five pence coin held up twenty feet away. Amazingly, what at first glance looked like hundreds of stars was in fact thousands of galaxies, each containing hundreds of billions of stars. It's an incredible photo, showing the immense size of the known universe. It not only shows the number of galaxies but also that these galaxies are different shapes. Firstly, there are spiral galaxies, like a Catherine wheel in a fireworks display, dominated by a central spherical bulge on a disc with spiral arms, which extend outward from the nucleus in a spiral pattern resembling a celestial pinwheel. These are the most conducive to life. Secondly, there are elliptical galaxies which are sort of egg shaped. Here, stars tend to be too metal-poor and have evolved into giants that are too old and hot for life on inner planets. They are not favourable for life. Thirdly, there are irregular galaxies which appear disorganised and distorted, not having the order necessary for stable orbits. These are hostile to complex life.

Unsurprisingly, the Milky Way Galaxy in which we live is spiral. It is mostly a flat disc spanning one hundred thousand light years across, with a bulge in the middle where several hundred billion stars rotate around a monster black hole called Sagittarius A*. Where we are located is important. The Milky Way is not in a cluster of galaxies, if it were, the gravitational force from the cluster itself would rip us apart. Our nearest galaxy is Androm-eda (which is hurtling towards us at 250,000 miles per hour and might bring about our eventual doom) but we are far enough away to have a stable environment for life. The thin disc and relative flatness of our galaxy helps our sun stay in its desirable circular orbit, preventing it from crossing spiral arms and entering either the dangerous inner area or the outer regions of the galaxy.

The black hole at the centre of the Milky Way is more than four million times the mass of the sun. This along with a mass of gas and clusters of deadly neutron stars that eject lethal amounts of radiation. So, towards the centre of our galaxy the environment is hostile and antagonistic to life. Alternatively, at the edge of the Milky Way the composition changes. Heavier elements, which are needed to form Earth-like planets, occur more towards the centre of the galaxy, so it is less likely to have Earth-type planets that are beneficial to life at the periphery.

Our sun is about 25,000 light years (around halfway) from the centre, and in this position we slowly orbit the central axis of the galaxy. Like a planet revolving around a star, we maintain roughly the same distance from the galactic centre. This is called the galactic habitable zone, that slight area within our galaxy that is favourable to life. Even there:

> Ironically, (because of binary or multiple star systems, wrong types of stars, wrong age of star or clusters of stars) most areas within the galactic habitable zone aren't all that liveable.[96]

Yet, here we are, within the narrow zone where life sustaining planets are possible. As Professor Brian Cox said recently, in an interview on *The Joe Rogan Experience*, 'We are probably the

---

[96] Hugh Ross, *Why the Universe is the Way it is?*, 2008, p. 67

only complex life in this galaxy.'[97] He has hope for other galaxies though.

A SPECIFIC SUN

When you look up to the sky on a clear night you could understandably conclude that our sun is one of trillions of other stars that could form a stable energy source to make a habitable planet possible. But this would be wrong. Only 90% of all stars are 'main sequence stars', meaning that they are at the right age of their life, neither being born nor dying, but a good middle age to be stable enough for the long haul of life. But that is still a lot, yes, but the sun is not just at the right age in its life, but the right type of star. It is technically called a G-type main-sequence star, or a yellow dwarf star, which means it is larger than most. Just 2.7%[98] of main sequence stars are G-type yellow dwarfs. M-dwarfs, or red dwarfs are by far the most common type of star in the Milky Way. This isn't just splitting hairs in classification because they are very different stars. Red dwarfs are smaller and cooler which means that 80% of all stars are less conducive for life, which makes our planetary system quite rare.

You can be sure that none of the stars that you see in the night sky are red dwarfs because their light is drastically fainter. Our nearest star, Proxima Centauri is just 4.2 light years away and yet if we were in the southern hemisphere, you could not see it with the naked eye. For stars like red dwarfs, which are smaller than the sun, the planet needs to be closer to the star for heat and

---

[97]   See the full interview at *www.youtube.com/watch?v=wieRZoJSVtw*
[98]   Professor David Kipping, Assistant Professor of Astronomy at Columbia University, *https://www.youtube.com/watch?v=TAQKJ4leDTs*

that means the habitable zones are located further inward. But then gravitational tidal effects from the star can cause a synchronous rotation for the planet, meaning the same side of the planet always faces the star. This leads to extreme conditions: the dark side of the planet freezes, and the light side roasts. If our sun was a red dwarf there would be further problems: photosynthesis would be made more difficult because it emits red light, not yellow; extreme flares combined with our need to be close would leave us exposed to radiation that would wipe us out. Red dwarfs also produce very little UV light, something that is necessary early in the process in order to build up the oxygen that is essential for complex life. They tend to be more erratic and less stable, having far more solar flares and emissions from their surfaces. These flares have the protentional to strip a planet's atmosphere.

About half of all G-Type stars live in binary orbits; we have a bachelor. Our 'sun is not only the right mass, but it also emits the right colours; a balance of red and blue.'[99] Our sun is metal-rich, having an abundance of heavy elements compared to other stars of its age in this region of the galaxy. Our sun is highly stable, more so than most comparable stars. Recent studies by Ron Gilliland[100] in 2011 and Timo Reinhard[101] in 2020 have shown that our sun is unusually quiet, meaning, stable in its energy output. This prevents wild climate swings on Earth. To sum up, our sun has the right mass, the right light, and the right composition; it is at the right distance from Earth, it has the right orbit, in the right

[99] Peter Ward, Donald Brownlee, *Rare Earth; Why Complex Life is Uncommon in the Universe?*, 2004, p. 23–4

[100] Ronald Gilliland (and others), 'KEPLER MISSION STELLAR AND INSTRUMENT NOISE PROPERTIES', *https://arxiv.org/pdf/1107.5207.pdf*

[101] Timo Reinhold (and others), 'The Sun is less active than other solar-like stars', *https://arxiv.org/pdf/2005.01401.pdf*

type of galaxy, at the right location in this galaxy to nurture living organisms on a circulating planet and it has been estimated that less than 0.5% of G-type stars are like our own. That is rare.

OUR COSMIC HOOVER: THE OUTER PLANETS

It is said that an astronomer's worst fear is that he might be called an astrologer. Astrology suggests that the stars and planets exert a major influence on our daily life. While this is mysticism, recent research has, in an odd way, proved astrologers slightly correct. Two types of heavenly bodies, the moon and our outer planets, do in fact play pivotal roles in our very existence as a species.

Our solar system is made up of inner and outer planets that orbit the Sun. Mercury, Venus, Earth, and Mars make up the inner solar system. Then we have an asteroid belt, before heading out to the outer planets of Jupiter, Saturn, Uranus, and Neptune (with Pluto either a part of it or not). The thing to notice is that almost all these planets have a near circular orbit. Earth's orbit is 'almost' a perfect circle. Without these outer, larger planets, the orbit of the inner ones would be less stable, and the temperature shifts on the surface of the planet would cause ice ages. The sustained circular orbit that is necessary to maintain a relatively steady temperature is only possible because Jupiter's orbit isn't very elliptical, and therefore doesn't threaten to distort our circular orbit.

Jupiter is a giant gas bowl that gets hotter and denser with depth. Even using a small backyard telescope, Jupiter is quite a sight. Ten times larger than Earth and over three hundred times its mass, it is by far the most massive planet orbiting the Sun.

Because it is so dense, it exerts enormous gravitational influence, and this is amazingly effective in scattering any approaching bodies. According to George Weatherall of the Carnegie Institute of Washington, the amount of ten kilometre-wide bodies hitting the Earth might be 10,000 times higher if Jupiter had not come into being. This means Earth might have been subject to collisions from extinction level projectiles every 10,000 years, instead of every 100 million years, and complex life would be unlikely to survive. When planetary systems lack planets to guard the outer boundary of the terrestrial planet region, the inner planets may not be capable of supporting more than microbial life. Ours has two of these 'cosmic vacuums', Jupiter and Saturn.

OUR FAITHFUL FRIEND: THE MOON

Finding a planet out there is only one part of the equation for life. We need a moon. There are an incredible two-hundred-and-five moons in our own solar system, but none like our own. The moon is just a spherical rock 2,000 miles in diameter and 250,000 miles away, but its presence has enabled Earth to become a long-term habitable planet. The moon is a fascinating factor in the rare Earth concept because the likelihood that an Earth-like planet should have such a large moon is small. The conditions suitable for moon formation were common for the outer planets but rare for the inner ones. The only moons of terrestrial inner planets in our solar system are ours and Phobos and Deimos, the two tiny moons of Mars that measure only ten kilometres in diameter. Our moon is something of an anomaly because of its large size in comparison to its parent planet. At nearly one third the size of Earth, in some ways it is more of a twin than a subordinate.[102] This unique size stabilizes Earth's axis. Earth's tilt is 23.5 degrees, giving us very mild seasons. Without the moon, the tilt angle would wander in response to the gravitational pulls of both the Sun and Jupiter, swinging wildly over a large range and resulting in major temperature swings between the extremes of the Sahara and the Antarctic. Instead, because the gravity from the moon's orbit keeps it stabilised, it has only a tiny variation of 1.5 degrees. As Astronomer Jacques Laskar says, 'We owe our present climate stability to an exceptional event; the presence of the moon.'[103] The moon fuels our tides, contributing to 60% of our tidal system, with the sun accounting for the other 40%. You can detect the sea 'breath in and out' morning and evening as we rotate here on Earth. It bulges, as the moon's gravitational effect is realised. When the moon and sun align every two weeks this increases the tidal swell. Tides serve an important role by flushing out nutrients from the continents to the oceans, which keeps them more nutrient rich than they would otherwise be. The moon also slows down our Earth's rotation. If it was bigger, it would slow down the Earth too much, meaning days would become too long and the temperature differences between night and day would be too extreme. The moon is exactly the right size and in exactly the right place to help create a habitable environment for Earth. Interestingly, the moon is now generally believed to have formed as a consequence of a glancing collision with a Mars-sized body during the later stages of the Earth's

---

[102] Peter Ward, Donald Brownlee, *Rare Earth*, 2004, p. 222
[103] *ibid*, p. 224

formation.[104] If such moon-forming collisions are rare, habitable planets might be equally as rare. As Brownlee and Ward say:

> Of the many elements of the rare Earth hypothesis, the presence of our huge moon seems to be one of the most important and yet most perplexing. Without the large moon . . . it seems most unlikely that life could have progressed as successfully as it has.[105]

THE SAFE ZONE: THE CHZ

The precise placement of Earth within what is called the Circumstellar Habitable Zone (CHZ) results in a climate that is warm enough, yet also allows for liquid water on the surface. This balance is determined by the distance from the host star and the amount of light it provides. Too close, and water evaporates into the atmosphere, causing a runaway greenhouse effect and boiling off the oceans. Too far out and water and carbon dioxide freeze, eventually leading to runaway glaciation. As you go further from the sun the carbon dioxide content of the planet's atmosphere must increase to trap the sun's radiation and keep water liquid. It's only in the very inner edge of this habitable zone that you can have a low enough carbon dioxide level and high enough oxygen levels to sustain complex animal life. A couple of percent either way spells disaster. Too close, we burn. Too far away, we freeze.

[104] Marcus Chown, *The Ascent of Gravity*, 2017, p. 57
[105] *ibid*, p. 234

LIFE'S BASIC SOLVENT

Complex life requires the presence of a solvent that can provide a medium for chemical reactions, transporting molecules to reaction sites whilst preserving their integrity. This solvent should be a liquid as the solid state doesn't allow for mobility, and the gaseous state prevents sufficiently frequent reactions. Further, the solvent should be liquid over the same range of temperatures where the basic molecules of life remain largely intact and in the liquid or gaseous state. Water, the most abundant chemical compound in the universe, exquisitely meets all these needs and requirements.

Water is virtually unique in being denser as a liquid than a solid. As a result, ice floats in water, insulating the water underneath from further loss of heat. This simple fact prevents lakes and oceans freezing from the bottom up. Water moves from solid to liquid to gas easily, helping to moderate Earth's climate. Liquid water has a surface tension which is higher than that of almost all other liquids, this gives it better capillary action in soils, trees and circulatory systems and a greater ability to form discreet structures with membranes. Finally, water is essential for maintaining Earth's plate tectonics, which is an all-important part of our climate regulation system.

It is striking that so many unique qualities should occur together in one substance. For water to fulfil all these distinct functions, a planet's water supply must *be large enough* to sustain a sizeable ocean on the surface, which must *not be lost to space* and must *exist in liquid form*. This is what we have on this privileged planet.

LIFE'S BASIC ELEMENT

As I have said, I am a big fan of anything sci-fi. Often, in our sci-fi stories, the brave heroes meet aliens from other worlds, whose different appearance is the result of being a species based on a different element. The reality is that, as far as scientists can tell, this universe seems to be carbon-based. Silicone-based life, or life based on any other element, just won't happen. Carbon atoms form the 'backbone' of almost all the important biological molecules floating around in our bodies (except water, of course.) When we say life is 'carbon based', we mean that our skin, hair and cells are all made from molecules that contain large amounts of carbon. This 'building block' must be stable enough to withstand significant chemical and thermal conditions but not so stable that it won't react with other molecules at low temperatures. In other words, it must be metastable. Carbon excels in this regard. It forms gases when combined with oxygen and, most importantly, when other key atoms are added to carbon, we get the informational backbone (DNA) and the building blocks of life (amino acids). Carbon gives these molecules an information storage capacity that vastly exceeds any of the alternatives. In fact, the half-dozen or so key chemical requirements for life are rare or absent in other elements but are all present in carbon. This 'exactness' and its abundance in this universe and on Earth is a startling fact to some scientists. In fact, for life to exist on Earth an abundant supply of carbon is needed. Carbon is formed either by combining three helium nuclei, or by combining nuclei of helium and beryllium. Eminent mathematician and astronomer, Sir Fred Hoyle, found that for this to happen, the nuclear ground state energy levels must be fine-tuned with respect to each other.

This phenomenon is called resonance. If the variation were more than 1% either way, the universe could not sustain life. Hoyle later confessed that nothing had shaken his atheism as much as this discovery. Even this degree of fine tuning was enough to persuade him that it looked as if 'a super intellect has monkeyed with the physics as well as the chemistry and biology' and that 'there are no blind forces in nature worth talking about'."[106]

Biochemist A. E. Needham comments, 'As in so many other respects, carbon seems to have the best of both worlds, combining stability with pliability, momentum with inertia.' Biologist Michael Denton, in arguing that the weak chemical bonds which allow a large organic molecule to form three-dimensional shapes, an essential for the requirement for life, says:

> Nearly all the biological activities of virtually all the large molecules in the cell are critically dependent on their possessing very precise 3D shapes. Nature has provided no other glue to hold together the molecule superstructure of the cell. While we cannot have carbon-based life in the cosmos without covalent bonds, as there would be no molecules, just as certainly, we cannot have carbon-based life without these weak non-covalent bonds, because the molecules would not have stable 3D complex shapes.[107]

John Lewis, a planetary scientist at the University of Arizona, agrees that carbon and water have no equals. After considering possible alternatives he concludes:

[106] John Lennox, *God's Undertaker*, 2009, p. 70.
[107] Michael Denton, *Natures Destiny*, 1998, p. 114

despite our best efforts to step aside from the terrestrial chauvinism and to seek out other solvents and structural chemistries for life, we are forced to conclude that water is the best of all possible solvents and carbon compounds are apparently the best of all possible carriers of complex information.

OUR AIR CONDITIONER: THE ATMOSPHERE

Let's take a breath for a minute and consider how breathing is even possible. Our atmosphere is a layer or a set of layers of gases surrounding a planet that is held in place by the gravity of the Earth. It is composed mostly of nitrogen (about 78%), and oxygen (about 21%) with argon (about 0.9%), carbon dioxide (0.13%) and other gases in trace amounts. Oxygen is used by most organisms for respiration development, and 'typically the more advanced the life-form the more atmospheric oxygen it needs to thrive.'[108] Nitrogen is fixed by bacteria and lightning to produce ammonia used in the construction of nucleotides and amino acids. Carbon dioxide is used by plants, algae, and cyanobacteria for photosynthesis. The atmosphere helps to protect living organisms from genetic damage by solar ultraviolet radiation, solar wind and cosmic rays.

Earth's ability to *regulate its climate* hinges on carbon dioxide and water vapour and, to a lesser extent, methane, all of which are important atmospheric greenhouse gases. These vapours, essential for life, are freely exchanged amongst our planet's living

[108]   Hugh Ross, *Improbable Planet*, 2017, p. 119

creatures, atmosphere, oceans and solid interior. Together they create a unified climate feedback system and have kept Earth a lush planet. It's hard to ignore the intricate link between the planetary environment and the chemistry of life.[109] We have a unique, oxygen-rich atmosphere that protects us from outside threats while allowing us to thrive within it.

WHAT LIES BENEATH: THE CORE

What makes Earth different from the other planets in our solar system? Why can Earth sustain life? As we have said, Earth is unique in its possession of liquid water at the surface, its oxygen rich atmosphere, its temperature range which allows liquid water to exist and its linear mountain ranges. At this crude level of observation, oceans, mountain ranges and atmosphere set Earth apart in the solar system.

These attributes of Earth are connected in a complex inter-dependent relationship and all three may be the result of plate tectonics caused by our planet's core. These plate movements do several things. Firstly, plate tectonics *promotes high levels of global biodiversity*. High biodiversity is the major defence against mass extinction. Secondly, plate tectonics *provides a global thermostat* by recycling chemicals that keep the volume of carbon dioxide in our atmosphere relatively uniform—this has been the single most important mechanism enabling liquid water to remain on Earth's surface. Thirdly, plate tectonics is the *dominant force that causes changes in sea level*, which, it turns out, are vital to

---

[109] Peter Ward, Donald Brownlee, *Rare Earth*, 2004, p. 36

the formation of minerals that keep the level of global carbon dioxide in check. Fourthly, plate tectonics *created the continents*, without which planet Earth may only be a watery world with isolated volcanic islands dotting its surface. Fifthly, plate tectonics makes possible one of the Earth's most potent defence systems, its *magnetic field*. A strong magnetic field contributes mightily to a planet's habitability by creating a cavity called the magnetosphere, which protects our atmosphere from direct interaction with the solar wind. If solar winds were to interact more directly with the Earth's upper atmosphere, they would be much more effective at stripping it away. For life, that would be bad news, since water would be lost far more quickly to space. Earth's magnetic field serves as the next line of defence against galactic cosmic ray particles after the sun's magnetic field and solar wind deflect the lower energy cosmic rays. This is amazing. So much so that Owen Gingerich, professor emeritus of astronomy and of the history of science at Harvard University and a senior astronomer emeritus at the Smithsonian Astrophysical Observatory says:

> I am personally persuaded that a super intelligent creator exists beyond and within the cosmos, and that the rich context of congeniality shown by our universe, permitting and encouraging the existence of self-conscious life, is part of the creator's design and purpose.[110]

---

[110] Owen Gingerich, *God's Universe* quoted in David Robertson, *The Dawkins Letters*, 2010, p. 75

WHAT SHALL WE SAY TO THESE THINGS?[111]

Let's piece this all together; we are in both the right size and type of galaxy, at the right point of time and in the exact position in the galaxy conducive to life. We have the right host star, not a binary, but one star. Our sun is the right size, has the right type of light and its age and distance from us are quite perfect. We have giant outer planets, like cosmic bouncers, which protect us from planet-killing projectiles. We have a moon big enough and near enough to give us stability, maintain tidal control and keep our tilt stable. Our Earth's atmosphere is uniquely able to maintain a heat balance yet filter harmful UV rays. It is oxygen-rich and maintained by a specific carbon cycle. We have life's basic solvent, water, in abundance, together with life's basic element, carbon. The core of our planet is a molten furnace which gives us continents, stabilises sea levels that create global biodiversity, provides a global thermostat, and produces a magnetic field to guard off harmful cosmic rays.

So how does all this happen? Is it possible that all this intricately balanced precision came about by chance? The probability is exponentially low. This planet is a cosy *pale blue dot* in the almost infinite black, hostile ocean of this universe, that is habitable.[112] It stands unique and that is staggering. This is my judge-

---

[111] Romans 8:31

[112] In the back of your mind, you are probably thinking about the question of extraterrestrial life. As far as we can tell, the make up of our universe is consistent throughout. I think, then, life in the simple form of amino acids and the like (the building blocks), might be found. However, in this I am agnostic. Anyway, there is an exponential gap between simple life and complex intelligent life (a gap I don't think is taken seriously enough!). If you are wondering about the presence of this complex life, I stand with physicist Enrico Fermi in asking the question, 'If there is complex life out there, why have they not visited?'

ment; this is not meaningless, and it makes us privileged. On my wife's finger is a *pale diamond dot*. It is small in terms of size, but not in terms of value. I think this is true of Earth.

We have a *Rare Earth*,[113] but this is only a fraction of the ingredients needed for life. Paul Davies reminds us that we must take this further as he says there are *two* basic requirements for complex life. The first is an Earth-like planet, that we have looked at, but the second is the genesis of life:

> The fact that a planet is habitable, is not the same as saying it is inhabited . . . suppose the emergence of life from life is a freak affair, an event of such low probability that even with a trillion, trillion habitable planets it would still be unlikely to happen more than once? The sheer size of the universe would then count for little if the odds are so heavily stacked against the spontaneous formation of life.[114]

There are not a trillion, trillion planets that are suitable for life. Far, far from it. Earth is rare. But even if there were, the deeper, infinitely greater challenge is the origin of complex life. Put these two aspects together and you can see the utter uniqueness of our situation: having both this planet and the genesis of life. That is the subject of our next chapter, the complex cell.

---

[113] This is the title of Ward and Brownlee's book, *Rare Earth*, 2004
[114] Paul Davies, *The Eerie Silence*, 2011, p. 24

CHAPTER 5

THE COMPLEX CELL

*Where the cosmos feels infinitely large,
and the atomic realm infinitely small;
the cell feels infinitely complex.*[115]

Michael Denton

When we are confronted with complexity that outstrips anything we could fabricate, it is hard to fight[116] the intuitive sense that the world we live in is designed. Man has always noticed this and naturally inferred upwards to some designer. 'Suppose I find a watch upon the ground,' says William Paley:

> The watch must have had a maker . . . who formed it for
> the purpose . . . who comprehend its construction and
> designed its use . . . every manifestation of design, which
> existed in the watch, exists in the works of nature. The

---

[115] Michael Denton, *Miracle of the Cell*, 2020, p. 16
[116] When reading a lot of the material, Francis Crick, who won the Nobel Prize jointly with James Watson for the discovery of the double helix structure of DNA, warns biologists not to mistake that impression for what it is, in his estimation, the underlying reality 'biologists must constantly keep in mind that what they see was not designed, but rather evolved', accrediting 'laws' with divine power or purpose.

difference on the side of nature is of being greater or more, and that in a degree which exceeds all computation.[117]

Simply put, he says that the sheer intricacy and irreducible complexity of the watch intuitively makes him think upwards to an intelligence, it naturally implies the existence of a watchmaker. He goes on to say:

> The marks of design are too strong to be got over. Design must have a designer. That designer must have been a person. That person is God.

Although Paley has been much maligned for the simplicity of his idea,[118] it seems that there is power to his argument. Not only has it convinced many, but as 'faithful' atheists continue to ask, 'How is this universe so finely tuned and complex?', it becomes clear that 'arguing power of design' continues to nag at the back of their minds. In his book, Dennis Alexander tells of a lady in his church who became a Christian from a completely atheistic background.

> [She] had become convinced there must be a God while sitting through a standard university biochemistry lecture, hearing the amazing story of how two metres (about six feet) of DNA are packed into a single cell.'[119]

[117] *Natural Theology or Evidences of the Existence and Attributes of the Deity*, 18th ed. Rev. Edinburgh, Lackington, Allen and Co., and James Sawers, 1818, pp. 12–14, quoted John Lennox, 2009, *God's Undertaker*, p. 80–81

[118] Richard Dawkins, *The Blind Watch Maker*, 2016. You should not only read his book—he is a genuinely good writer—but read a review of it in, *The Naked Emperor*, Antony Latham, 2005. In chapter 15, he shows the real weakness of the book.

[119] Denis Alexander, *Creation or Evolution*, 2008, p. 62

Do you see that power to convince? That gut feeling that when we see complexity we look upward? Dr Gene Myers, the computer scientist who worked on genome mapping at the Maryland headquarters of Celera Genomics, said, 'We are deliciously complex at the molecular level . . . There's still a metaphysical, magical element . . . It's like it was designed . . . there is a huge intelligence there. I don't see that as being unscientific. Others may, but not me.'[120] Additionally, Dr Allan Sandage, the American astronomer who determined the first reasonably accurate values for the Hubble constant[121] and the age of the universe, in discussing his conversion to Christianity at the age of fifty said:

> The world is too complicated in all its parts and interconnections to be due to chance alone. I am convinced that the existence of life with all its order and each of its organisms is simply too well put together.[122]

I think they are right. Life 'seems' to be designed, yet in the scientific world it appears you must fight against the impulse to believe it. This becomes problematic when describing the universe. Listen to biologists and cosmologists try to find words to illustrate its intricacy: cells are referred to as mini cities full of complexity, proteins are said to be mini machines, the universe is fine-tuned and DNA is like a computer software language. All these descriptions of life point to something or someone behind the curtain. A city is planned out, machines are manufactured,

[120] John Lennox, *God's Undertaker*, 2009, p. 176
[121] Hubble's law is the observation in physical cosmology that galaxies are moving away from the Earth at speeds proportional to their distance.
[122] Allan Sandage, *A Scientist Reflects on Religious Belief, Truth* 1, 1985, p. 54

dials are tuned and language originates in minds, but still we are told to resist and push back against the apparently primitive and archaic idea of design. We still, it seems, 'cannot allow the divine foot in the door.'[123]

It is true that certain levels of complexity can develop under forces, like the tunnel of a tornado or the whirlpool of water running out of a bath, but no force can create complexity and order on the level that we will look at now. This is a different degree altogether. A star which is formed through gravitational pull, although filled with power, is not alive. We, on the other hand, are alive and complexity fills us. There is a wealth of difference isn't there?

Watch some of Drew Berry's amazing animations describing the process of proteins working[124] and try not to think there is design in that kind of complexity. Or listen to a lecture from Ron Vale, then dictate the process of the workings of a cell to any engineer, and he is likely to talk in terms of a design and shop floor. If you watch a video of a Neutrophil chasing down bacteria,[125] and I encourage you to do so, you will see that it is just a tiny speck of matter, invisible to the naked eye, so small that a hundred of them could be lined up across the top of a pen. But it is seemingly endowed with intention and agency to hunt, like a cat chasing a mouse, or a kind of biological Pacman. For any thinking person, that will be startling. It senses the chemical aroma of the bacterium and crawls in a specific direction to hunt it down. These skills are remarkable at any time, but when we find them on the molecular level, we sit back in awe at the 'miracle' of

---

[123] Richard Lewontin, *Billions and Billions of Demons*, NY *Review of Books* (7 January 1997)

[124] See video: *https://www.youtube.com/watch?v=7Hk9jct2ozY*

[125] See video: *https://www.youtube.com/watch?v=Z_mXDvZQ6dU*

biology. Understanding how this happens doesn't take away from the wonder of it, or the impression of design, any more than the understanding of how a Lamborghini Miura works takes away from the thrill of it or the fact that it was designed by Marcello Gandini. If anything, understanding how it works makes us appreciate the genius of Marcello. It certainly doesn't give me the right to take him out of the equation altogether.

In a conversation with a friend who had recently come to faith, I asked him, 'How would you try to convince people to believe in God?' Without hesitation he replied, 'Show them nature.' It seems to me that if we throw off Paley's argument too quickly, we might lose out. If there is a Designer or Watchmaker, then design might be part of His grand evidence, built into this universe for us.

THE COMPLEX CELL

If you have ever looked at a cell under a microscope you will have seen a world of complexity. It is like one of those aerial drone shots of a city with its vast network of roads and railway tracks or even air routes, the production and destruction of buildings and a multitude of pieces working together to grow, multiply and develop the city itself. It is a dizzying sight to behold. Take a simple cell and put it under a high-powered electron microscope and you will see something very similar. A city-like complex structure with production, destruction, transport and exchange of information, with all its parts working together in an exact dance-like symmetry. As Paul Davies says:

> The living cell is the most complex system known to man. Vastly more complicated than the most complicated ballet,

the dance of life encompasses endless molecular perform-
ers in synergetic coordination.[126]

These complex cells are the basic unit of life. Everything is made
of them because 'all living organisms, regardless of their size or
complexity, emerge from a cell.'[127] They come in an incredible
variety of shapes and sizes. Most of them are truly minute—too
small to be seen with the naked eye. The parasitic bacterium
that can infect the bladder could be lined up three thousand
abreast across a one-millimetre gap. Other cells are immense. If
you had an egg for breakfast, its yolk is just one single cell. In our
bodies, there are individual nerve cells that reach from the base
of your spine all the way to the tip of your big toe; that's about a
metre long. Cells are made up of trillions of atoms, representing
the complexity of a jumbo jet and more, all packed into a space
less than a millionth of the volume of a typical grain of sand. But
unlike any jumbo jet, unlike any nanotech, this wondrous entity
can replicate itself. This is a phenomenal aspect of a cell's makeup.
Biochemist Michael Denton says:

> Here is an 'Infinity machine' with seemingly magical
> powers. In terms of compressed complexity, cells are
> without peer in the material world, actualised or imagined.
> And there is likely far more complexity still to uncover. [128]

[126] Paul Davies, *The Origin of Life*, 1998, quoted in Anthony Latham, *Naked Emperor*, 2005, p. 12
[127] Paul Nurse, *What is Life?*, 2020, p. 15
[128] Michael Denton, *Miracle of the Cell*, 2020, p. 16

Even one of the earliest of cells ever found, called an Archean chert, which was discovered not far from the town of Port Hedland in Australia, should not be dismissed as simple and primitive; it is still massively complex. Think about a cell's incomparable diversity in form. Contrast a neuron with a red blood cell, a skin cell with a liver cell, and an amoeboid leucocyte with a muscle cell. Complexity is one thing, but cells appear supremely fit to fulfil their role as the basic unit of biological life. E. coli, those tiny organisms in our guts right now, are adept at breaking down and digesting the food that we eat. Cells also move in many diverse ways. E.coli travels by the propeller-like action of the bacterial flagellum (we will think about that later), while others do so via the beating action of cilia. Some even creep and crawl. Some cells can survive desiccation for hundreds of years. Cells possess internal clocks and can measure the passage of time. They can sense electrical and magnetic fields and communicate via chemical and electrical signals. Some can encase themselves in an armour like skin. All can replicate themselves with seeming ease; some can even reconstruct themselves completely, from tiny fractions cut surgically from the cell. Cells are the universal constructors of life on Earth. In short, they can do almost anything, adopt almost any shape, and obey any order. They are perfectly adapted to their assigned task of creating a biosphere ripe for multi-cellular organisms like ourselves.[129]

Of all these different forms, and the many more that are found in the human body, every member of this fantastic zoo of diversity is built on the same canonical design. Just like an atom consists of several components, of electrons and protons etc. that make

---

[129]   *ibid*, pp. 16–18

up the whole, so too with biology's atom.[130] Most writers will divide the cell into three features that are crucial to its makeup: the cell wall, its energy production and the gene.

THE CELL WALL: AN INTRICATE SKIN

A critically important part of any cell is the skin, or cell membrane. Although just two molecules thick, this outer membrane forms a flexible wall or barrier that separates each cell from the hostile outside world. This barrier is crucial to protect the cell and give a safe setting for its processes to take place within it. In the same way that you could not survive without skin, no cell could survive without a membrane. This outer wall is a very complex piece of apparatus which carries out numerous functions, making it uniquely suited to fulfil this crucial role.

As I have said it is *remarkably thin.* If a typical cell was expanded to the size of a pumpkin, its membrane would be thinner than a sheet of paper. This remarkable thinness isn't just striking, it is essential to the cell function, allowing proteins (which on average are about the same thickness as the membrane) to span its width. This is crucial for transport, as water soluble substances are moved in and out of the cell in a very controlled way. This makes the skin *semi-permeable.* No cell could survive without some sort of membrane that was relatively impermeable to the flow of material in and out, yet makes it separate from the external environment. So, most cells have special gates or pores

[130] Paul Nurse, *What is Life?*, 2020, p. 7

through which myriads of small compounds and particles pass in and out, again in a highly controlled manner.

The remarkable fact that it is *self-organising* allows the membrane, because of its intrinsic chemical nature, to form automatically around the outer surface of the cell. This means the membrane has the ability to self-repair. It can readily close any hole or break that would allow the cell's contents to diffuse away. If its membrane was not self-organising, or if it had to be assembled piece by piece, the cell would encounter profound challenges. The self-organising nature of the membrane also facilitates the generation of a great variety of emergent structures including tubes, vesicles and various types of layered structures. It can even be an *electric insulator*, allowing an electric charge to be built up across the membrane. The cell's capacity to generate and maintain a charge across its membrane allows for the transmission of nerve impulses of neurons in animal nervous systems.

Do you get a slight sense of the complexity of this microscopic skin, essential to the cell, with its correct size, semi-permeability and self-organisational ability, generational diversity and electrical potential? This is an essential, intricate component of the cell.

ENERGY FROM CHEMISTRY WITH LITTLE ENTROPY: THE CELL METABOLISM

Cells and all life need energy. Energy to move, crawl, transport and reproduce. Generating energy is thus a core aspect of cell life. Nothing lives without energy. So, where does this energy come from?

The Earth is not a closed system; we get a lot of our energy from the sun's rays, which are absorbed by plants (through photosynthesis) to make glucose, which is a simple sugar. Then, when we humans eat animals or plants, our cells convert this glucose to energy. This is called cellular respiration. It is the process of turning glucose into something like a battery, or a pod of energy, like a wound-up spring ready to go, that can be transported and used in the body. This battery is called ATP: it is 'life's miracle fuel, a mini power-pack with a lot of punch. Like a battery, it can keep its energy stored until needed, then—*kerpow!*'[131] But, how?

This happens in three steps of the most sophisticated and advanced chemistry I have seen:[132] glycolysis, the (Krebs) citric acid cycle and finally the ETC and ATP synthase. The sum is that from the one original glucose molecule, 26–28 ATP 'batteries' are created to then power other parts of the cell. This is the chemistry of life.[133] Incredibly, you will produce your own body weight

---

[131] Paul Davies, *The Demon in the Machine*, 2019, p. 58

[132] Firstly, there is glycolysis. This happens in the cytoplasm of the cell where in ten amazing chemical steps, using ten different enzymes, one glucose molecule is broken down to two pyruvate molecules which produces two ATP molecules each. So, we have four batteries (ATP) after this stage. Then we have the (Krebs) citric acid cycle. The oxygen we breath in, is used to break down the pyruvate molecules. This happens in a compartment of the cell called the mitochondria, the engine of the cell. Through eight steps and another eight enzymes to produce three NADH, FADH2 and 1 ADP, this is multiped by two because of two pyruvates. Two ATP batteries are not enough, as 'a single cell consumes around a hundred million molecules of ATP every second' (Paul Nurse, *What is Life?*, 2020); our body needs a lot more. Enter the ETC and ATP synthase. This is where we get the big payoff producing energy. In the inner membrane of the mitochondria there are certain proteins that retain electrons in the inside but shuttle protons to the outside of the membrane from the newly created NADH and FADH. This creates a 'proton gradient', where protons gather on the outside of the membrane. Now enter ATP synthase, an amazing mini machine that is in the membrane. Protons enter this and like a stream of water turning a waterwheel, this mini machine is turned by the flow of protons joining with the ADP to create ATP molecules.

[133] Paul Nurse, *What is Life?*, 2020, Chapter 4

in ATP every day. On one level this is basic chemistry, but on another level, it is a complicated process: from the stripping down of a glucose molecule to changing, transporting and reusing the elements and forming energy through the action of proteins and enzymes. It is an intricate miracle of efficiency and complexity.

THE SUPER-COMPOSITE SHOP FLOOR: THE CELL GENE

When my second daughter was born, we had a couple of months of worry as she looked exactly like my wife's cousin, Jeff. Thankfully, she grew out of that quickly, taking on the closer, beautiful appearance of her mother and the impressive 'Hewitt' genes. She is growing into a beautiful young girl who can dazzle you and get away with most things because of her cuteness. There are similarities that run through a family, traits and characteristics that are shared and, although generations pass, relatedness is often still evident. How does this happen? It is down to the gene, the code that controls our heredity.

We know this through the work of Gregor Mendel and his many experiments, crossbreeding peas. He noticed differences from generation to generation, to which he postulated 'that inherited characteristics are determined by the presence of physical particles, which exist as a pair.'[134] This was ground-breaking and was developed by Walther Fleming, a German military physician, who observed for the first time a microscopic structure

---

[134]   *ibid.*, p. 26

that looked like tiny threads within the nucleus of the cell (see illustration[135]).

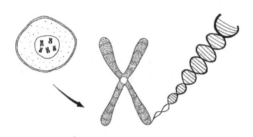

These threads are what we now call chromosomes, the physical structures that contain our genetic information. Every cell in our bodies contains these threads. We have forty-six: twenty-three from our father and twenty-three from our mother. This genetic code carries the essential information our cells need to replicate, maintain themselves and produce the building blocks for our bodies to live and thrive[136]. You might remember in the movie Jurassic Park, zoologists were able to take sucked up blood from a preserved mosquito, that had been feasting on dinosaurs, and read the genetic code like an instruction manual, using it to build a living, working T-Rex.

Each of these microscopic threads is really a wound up, unbroken line of DNA. These DNA strands can be exceptionally long for their minute size. Take the human chromosome number 2, which contains a string of 1,300 different genes. If you stretched

[135]   Illustration by Sarah Arrell
[136]   I am a visual learner, so if you want a two-minute video, go to *https://www.youtube. com/watch?v=URUJD5NEXC8*

96

it out, it would measure more than eight centimetres in length. In fact, if you were to take all forty-six chromosomes, the entire human genome, and stretch them out, it would come to just over two metres. It is, however, impressively well coiled up, as Paul Nurse explains:

> Through some miracle of packing, it all fits into a cell that measures no more than a few thousandths of a millimetre across. What is more, if you could somehow join it together and then stretch out all the DNA coiled up inside your body's several trillion cells into a single, slender thread, it'd be about 20 billion kilometres long. That's long enough to stretch from Earth to the sun and back sixty-five times.[137]

The sophistication of this system was visualised in 1953 when Watson and Crick won the race to understand the structure of this DNA molecule. They saw it like a ladder that is twisted to form a spiral. This helix structure helped biologists to understand how DNA can both encode the information and, secondly, replicate itself. The sheer wonder of this is that, if you rip the ladder in two, each of the rungs of the ladder is a kind of letter, or code, that contains the information for the programming of the body in four letters, A, C, G, and T, representing the different nucleotide bonds of adenine, cytosine, guanine and thymine. So, if your body needed a certain protein, how would it go about making it? Get ready for the complexity of the shop floor.

---

[137] Paul Nurse, *What is Life?*, 2020, p. 32

The histone that holds the DNA into a coil will release it so that little 'machines', really proteins, can attach themselves to it. They will split the ladder, read the code and transcribe it. Obviously, the code needs to be copied correctly so, amazingly, it is checked for errors by another little machine. It is then transported, by yet another machine, to a factory floor called a ribosome. Here the code is read three letters at a time. Each of these three letters, for example 'TGT' represents one of twenty-two different amino acids, TGT being 'cysteine'. As the code is read, and the different amino acids are added, it forms a chain like a pearl necklace. We are not finished yet. In an amazingly precise way, this neckless of amino acids is folded exactly to form the new protein. This process of making these 'mini-machines' is going on inside you at high-speed, millions of times a day. This is our microscopic super-composite shop floor, from instruction to production, and it is incredible.

'IT WAS THE BEST OF TIMES, IT WAS THE *BLURST* OF TIMES'

In one episode of *The Simpsons*, Mr Burns opens a door in his house to a room which, weirdly, is full of monkeys. They are sitting in rows, both smoking and working at typewriters. He goes over to one monkey, rips the sheet off the typewriter and reads it out: 'It was the best of times, it was the *blurst* of times.' Taken from Dickens, it should be 'It was the best of times, it was the worst of times.' 'Blurst of times, BLURST of times,' he starts shouting. 'You stupid monkey,' he screams. This scene is hilarious, as the odds of the monkey getting it anywhere near right are astronomical!

Now, think about what we have just talked through, the process of replicating one protein from that DNA code. Think of the odds of getting the code right for each of the amino acids that form the pearl necklace. Not just a sentence of twelve words, but a line of code three billion letters long. Fred Hoyle likened this happening by chance to a tornado blowing through a junkyard and forming a working 747 aeroplane. The sheer intricacy of the whole process is not just impressive, it is awe-inspiring. In fact, such is its awe-inspiring complexity that it brings a flood of difficulties—*how* did this level of intricacy come to be?

I say difficulties, but I do not mean 'proof texts' for design. In my mind, they have not yet been answered by our current scientific understanding. That's not to say they might not be answered someday, but, as yet, they present formidable difficulties that prevent a slow step by step climbing of 'mount improbable' from the simple beginning to the complexity of the cell. I am not talking about naturalistic evolution here, but the *complexity* and *origin* of the cell itself.

The first difficulty is *irreducible complexity*. I should say that, unfortunately, like Paley, the original proponent of this has been much maligned. I do agree 'there is a danger in concluding too readily that something is irreducibly complex'[138] as it could mean people giving up scientific pursuits in that area. But it seems to me that even Darwin himself saw the force of this, when he wrote:

> If it could be demonstrated that any complex organ existed
> which could not possibly have been formed by numerous,

---

[138]   Lucas and Pfundner, *Think God, Think Science*, 2008, p. 69

successive, slight modifications, my theory would abso-
lutely break down.[139]

Then I think there is serious weight behind this argument. Richard Dawkins wrote a book called *Climbing Mount Improbable*, in
which he describes the process of going from simple to complex
as a gradual step by step, inch by inch movement up the gentle
side of the mountain, until you reach the complex top. But what
if the cell, and certain components within it that are core to its
functioning, cannot come about step by step, inch by inch?

Let's think of a mouse trap, and its different components. First,
there's the flat wooden platform to which all the other parts are
attached. Second, there's a metal hammer, which does the job of
crushing the mouse. Third, there's the spring. Fourth, there's a
catch that releases when a mouse applies a slight bit of pressure.
Fifth, there's a metal bar that connects to the catch and holds the
hammer back when the trap is charged. If you take any of these
parts away, like the spring or the holding bar, the mouse trap
doesn't become half as efficient as it used to be or catch half as
many mice. It doesn't catch any mice: it's broken. It doesn't work
at all. Not only do all five parts have to be working, but they must
also be matched and have the right special relationship with each
other.[140] You can see the principle.[141]

---

[139] Charles Darwin, *The Origin of Species*, 6th edition, 1998, p. 154
[140] Michael Behe, *Darwin's Black Box*, 2007; also Lee Strobel, *The Case for a Creator*, 2004, p. 198
[141] For your entertainment, you should look up a comical version of the evolution of the mouse trap itself by John McDonald and Alex Fidelibus, or Joachim L. Dagg trying to attach Michael Behe, the original proponent of 'irreducible complexity': https://udel.edu/~mcdonald/mousetrap.html

Now, think about something like flagellum, the tiny acid-driven motor which was discovered in 1973. It is a propeller-like device that enables bacteria to swim.[142]

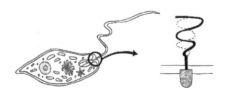

This motor is so small that 35,000 laid end-to-end would take up only one millimetre. It consists of some forty protein parts including a rotor, a stator, bushings and a driveshaft. If any one of these major protein parts was taken out, it would result in a complete loss of motor function. Like the mouse trap, the motor is irreducibly complex. It is a 'single system composed of several well matched, interacting parts the contribute to the basic function, we're in the removal of any one of the parts causes the system to effectively cease functioning.'[143] To my mind, none of the theories of how this may have come together come close to explaining this phenomenal complexity.[144] Take cilium, the whip-like hairs on the surface of cells which, if they are *fixed* in their location move fluid across the surface of the cell. I have a cold at the moment, and I am certainly ejecting plenty of fluid from my mouth and nose. Cilia do this by waving back and forth like

142   Illustration by Sarah Arrell
143   Michael Behe, *Darwin's Black Box*, 2007, p. 255–72
144   You should read Behe's own response which is thoughtful and has weight in its argument, *ibid*.

rowers on a boat, moving the mucus out. If a cilium is *mobile*, it can row through fluid.[145]

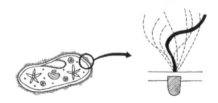

This sounds simple until you see it under an electron microscope, and then it becomes exponentially complex. Each 'hair' has micro-tubes in its interior that are connected by an amazing mini-machine called dynein. They cause the tubes to slide, producing the movement of the entire cilia. This is a simplified version of an incredibly complex process. But in broad terms the tubes, the way they are linked together, and the mini-machine dynein are all needed for this to work. Take out one and the mousetrap fails.

Let's now think about the *whole cell* in its three necessary areas: the gene, its metabolism and its membrane. How the complete cell has come to be is a massive problem in biology. The geneticist, Paul Nurse, who among many things is the director of the Francis Crick Institute in London and shared a Nobel Prize in Physiology, neatly puts it like this:

> But which came first? Replicating DNA-based genes, protein-based metabolism, or enclosing membrane? In today's living organisms these systems form a mutually independent system that only works properly as a whole.

[145] Illustration by Sarah Arrell

DNA-based genes can only replicate themselves with the assistance of protein enzymes. But protein enzymes can only be built from the instruction held in the DNA. How can you have one without the other? Then there's the fact that both genes and metabolism rely on the cell's outer membrane to concentrate the necessary chemicals, capture energy and protect them from the environment. But we know that cells alive today use genes and enzymes to build their sophisticated membranes. It's hard to imagine how one of this crucial trinity of genes, protein and membranes could have come about on its own: if you take one element away, the whole system rapidly comes apart.[146]

To understand how these three elements come together is to understand the origin of 'life' itself. Although this has become a new area of study in recent years, it remains maybe *the* major biological mystery, for the sheer gulf between 'life' and 'non-life', even in its simplest form, is exponential. It has a complexity that outstrips anything humanity has conceived.

In 1953 Stanley Miller, supervised by Harold Urey, conducted a famous experiment which attempted to reproduce the first complex life on the primordial Earth.[147] He was able to make a couple of amino acids through a highly 'designed' environment. This is still pointed to as a proof text of the creation of life. But as any biochemist will tell you, this is an exponential step from actual life.

[146] Paul Nurse, *What is Life?*, 2020, p. 203
[147] Stephen Meyer, *Signature in the Cell*, 2009, Ch. 2

There is no good explanation for how this complexity of life has come to be. There are theories for how life develops, but not for how life started. Some of these ideas seem a little like modern alchemy as 'there is a big gap in understanding the development from inorganic chemicals to the first living cell. There are a few possibilities . . . but this may just be straws in the wind.'[148] Whether it is clay surface, or tiny compartments in the early rock, or the RNA first model; it may be that some of these ideas have weight and should definitely be investigated to their conclusion, but it seems, by the admission of each author I have read that this is thin theoretical ice. David Berliski says that 'a great many people have concluded that when it comes to the origins of life, the [Hoyles 747] junkyard is all that Darwin offered'[149]. Hubert Yockey, the renowned physicist who worked on the Manhattan Project has concluded that:

> An ancient protein such as 'cytochrome c' could be expected to arise by chance only once in 1044 trials. The image of an indefatigable but hopelessly muddled universe trying throughout all eternity to create a single biological molecule is very sobering.

It seems to me at least, that not only are components of life (flagellum, cilium, the making of amino acids etc.) but the very cell itself is irreducibly complex.

The second line of 'difficulty' is the *chicken and the egg* scenario. Which came first, the chicken that then laid an egg,

---

[148] Michael Pfundner and Ernest Lucas, *Think God, Think Science*, 2008, p. 77–78

[149] David Berlinski, *The Devil's Delusion*, 2009, p. 141

or an egg that hatched to become a chicken? Their difficulty in deciding which came first is that they are dependent upon one another; you cannot have one without the other. We will look at two problems of this kind.

Firstly, *the membrane or the gene?* Even the simplest of cells has a complex membrane and it is essential to give an environment that is 'safe' to perform its work. Anthony Latham says:

> Far too often I hear experts confidently postulate about the first cell membrane. They know that the first life had to have a protective coat to hold the DNA and all the incredibly sophisticated molecular machinery inside the bacteria. Some, including Schopf (who discovered the Apex Chert bacteria), suggest that the first, fledgling and replicating DNA was surrounded by a type of soap bubble. The membrane of a bacterium is however entirely different from a simple soap bubble in structure and these first cyanobacteria had the same dynamically complex cell membranes as modern cells do. The actual details of the membrane must be coded for in the DNA of the cell. It is a major problem for theorists of early life to imagine how the first DNA achieved such a code without first having the membrane around it. Such chicken and egg scenarios bedevilled the understanding of early life.[150]

You see what he is saying, which came first? This is a massive problem.

---

[150] Antony Latham, *The Naked Emperor*, 2005, p. 12–13

Secondly, *the protein or the* DNA? It is very important in all of this to realise that, although the DNA gives rise to the proteins, the replication of DNA itself cannot proceed without the existence of a number of proteins. Robert Shapiro, an acknowledged expert on DNA chemistry, says:

> DNA holds the recipe for protein construction. Yet that information cannot be retrieved or copied without the assistance of proteins. Which large molecule appeared first proteins (the chicken) or DNA (the egg)?[151]

Similarly, Stephen Meyer says:

> In prokaryotic cells, DNA replication involves more than 30 specialised proteins to perform tasks necessary for building and accurately copying the genetic molecule . . . DNA needs these proteins to copy the genetic information contained in DNA. But the proteins that copy the genetic information in DNA are themselves built from that information. This again poses what is, at the very least, a curiosity; the production of proteins requires DNA, but the production of DNA requires proteins.[152]

Can you see the difficulty? Paul Davies in his book, *The Origin of Life* says:

---

[151] Whitfield, *Origins of Life, Nature* 427, p. 674-6, 2004, quoted John Lennox, *God's Undertaker*, 2009, p. 139
[152] Stephen Meyer, *Signature in the Cell*, 2009, p. 132

A short nuclear acid sequence (i.e. the building of proteins) . . . would have no chance of containing the information needed to code for the copying enzymes that it needs. Complex genomes require reliable copying, unreliable copying requires complex genomes. Which came first?[153]

INSUR-'MOUNT IMPROBABLE'

So far we have thought about the 'difficulties' the complex cell brings. There are formidable hills to overcome, but I think there is something more insurmountable for climbing Mount Improbable. That is the enigma of *information*. On one level, DNA and the whole genome can be understood 'as chemical entities: stable collections of atoms that obeyed the laws of physics and chemistry,'[154] but this only goes so far. In series three of *Taskmaster*, Greg Davies set the celebrities the task of popping a collection of balloons on a washing line. The fastest to pop them would win. There were two types of balloons, normal round ones and the long ones you got in a packet as a kid, that no one played with. As Al Murray walked up to the task he said in an offhand comment, 'Huh, that looks like morse code.' He then proceeded to whack and wallop his way to completing the task. At the end of the task, it was revealed that he was right. The balloons were arranged in Morse code, and it said, 'Pop one balloon to win.' No one won.

Think of that for a moment; in the dashes and dots conveyed by the balloons, information was carried from the Taskmaster's mind to the audiences' minds. Information itself is not physical,

153   Paul Davies, *The Origin of Life*, 2003, p. 32
154   Paul Nurse, *What is Life?*, 2020, p. 33

it is an invisible and non-material thing. The carriers of information may well be visible—like the balloons in dots or dashes, or like a pen writing on paper—but the information itself is invisible.

> As you are reading this, photons bounce off the book and are received by your eye, converted into electrical impulses, and transmitted to your brain. Suppose you pass on some information from this book to a friend by word of mouth. The sound waves carry the information from your mouth to your friend's ear, from where they are converted into electrical impulses and transmitted into his brain. Your friend now has the information that originated in your mind, but nothing material has passed from you to your friend. The carriers of the information have been material, but the information itself is not material.[155]

So, what about DNA, is it information? Well, yes, every one of those letters, TGAC, forms a kind of Morse code that conveys instructions. It is a kind of language. Bill Gates in his book *The Road Ahead* wrote, 'DNA is like a computer program but far, far more advanced than any software ever created.' Richard Dawkins has spoken of it as a 'river of information'[156] proceeding out of Eden. This DNA is a coded language, containing the information that forms and designs all forms of life.

This is where this can only turn upwards. When we see any kind of language or code, whether that is markings on a cave wall, the words 'Marry Me?' written in the sand on the beach,

[155] John Lennox, *God's Undertaker*, 2009, p. 177–8
[156] Richard Dawkins, *River out of Eden*, 1995, p. 14

or a digital code, we automatically think that there is an intelligence behind it. So, where does this code come from? This is the real problem with just a naturalistic look at the universe. Paul Davies in his book, *Demon in the Machine*, sees this and makes the point that we need a new kind of physics because our current method of study only works on a naturalistic level. Does there come a point in our scientific search when naturalistic ways of understanding this universe just don't cut it? I think there is. For anytime we see information, we automatically infer upwards to a mind, to an intelligence. Should we not do the same when we see, in code form, the longest word ever recorded? This means that the cell is not just complex in its physical features but also at the level of information. So, I think we need to rethink Paley's watch and update it. On the other side of Silicon Valley's fence from Bill Gates, here is my Apple version . . .

> Imagine if you were walking along a beach and you came upon an 'Apple-watch'. You pick it up and look at it. You see the strap and the metal casing, You open it up to reveal the circuitry and the power source. You say, 'That looks complex.' You then take it home and connect it to your computer, and discover another world of complexity. It is not just a hardware product, but there is a software world that is line after line of code, the binary language written as the instructions for how the watch works.

Can you see that this adds to the complexity of the hardware of Paley's watch? It is not just the 'hardware' of life, stars, planets, animals, the cell membrane, the metabolism, a flagellum, in which we can perceive design, but it is in the 'software', that three billion letter-long word. This means that I am inferring a little more than Paley did: it is based not just on design, but on the nature of information. It seems that 'molecular biology provides the first clear, the first resonant, answer to Paley's question.'[157] Information naturally leads to intelligence. Where does this come from? It seems to me that, when you look at the complexity of the cell, and at the information it communicates, that life is more than the cell, or the atom. At the biological level, information is more than cellular. It infers a mind, a Watchmaker who certainly doesn't look to be blind.

In 2001, when the human genome was first brought together and codified, the announcement was made on the front garden of the White House. The then president, Bill Clinton, said, 'Today . . . we are learning the language in which God created life.'[158] Maybe so. It is 'almost as if the creator autographed every cell'[159] with a word so complex that it would make us look upwards. If Bill Gates is right, and it is software: who programmed it? I'm not sure chance could. That's about as improbable as Mr Burn's monkey room writing Dickens. Biophysicist Dean Kenyon, co-author of a definitive textbook on the origin of life, whose studies have led him to the conclusion that biological information has been designed, said

> If science is based on experience, then science tells us that the message encoded in DNA must have originated from an intelligent cause.[160]

[157] David Berlinski, *The Deniable Darwin*, 2009, p. 153
[158] Francis Collins, *The Language of God*, 2007
[159] Lee Strobel, *The Case for a Creator*, 2004, p. 224
[160] Quoted in Stephen Meyer, *Return of the God Hypothesis*, 2021. p. 182

CHAPTER 5

At the heart of this topic is the fundamental question, 'What is the origin of this complexity?' This is Paley's question, and it is our question. We are warned not to infer design, but I admit that is difficult in the face of such overwhelming complexity, and an 'anomaly' of information, which seems to transcend this physical world. Is complexity on this scale not always intertwined with intelligence? I think if there is a digital 'river out of Eden', then Eden may be a good place to look for its source.

CHAPTER 6

WHY SCIENCE WORKS

If it disagrees with experiment, it's wrong. In that simple statement is the key to science.

Richard Feynman

My old chemistry teacher, Dr Coulter, was a tall man with a full beard and a booming voice that he never raised. I still remember the experiment he used to teach us about reactions. He took a basin of water and threw in a blob of potassium, resulting in a bang that made us all jump back in fright. Potassium and water do not mix and, unless you are prepared for the violent reaction, I don't recommend that you try. On the surface, the conflict between science and religion is a kind of potassium and water reaction saga: if you mix them there will be trouble. While this perception is widely accepted, I do not believe it to be true. You will hear people say, 'I don't believe in God; I believe in science,' as if they are extreme alternatives. This is, once again, the 'Mr Science and Reason' philosophy we looked at in Chapter One. It has become the spirit of our age, concluding that because we have science, we don't need God. In, *The Atheist's Guide to Reality*, Alex Rosenberg gives a great example of this, saying:

> There's so much more to atheism than its knockdown arguments that there is no God. There is the whole rest of the worldview that comes along with atheism. It's a demanding, rigorous, breath-taking grip on reality, one that has been vindicated beyond reasonable doubt. It's called Science.[161]

Rosenberg's claim is that the supposed 'knockdown arguments', and science, leave no room for God. The inference is that, because we have science, the logical outcome is atheism. I don't want you to think me naïve; there is most assuredly a conflict, but the conflict is not between science and God. A lot of the time we are pushed to think they are opposites, that it is either God or the Big Bang,[162] God or the multiverse,[163] God or evolution,[164] and so on. I want to suggest that it is not as simple as a 'one or the other' possibility. If we understand science, in its origin, its history and the notable figures at its foundation, that will automatically bear this out. Equally, if we grasp what Christianity truly is, then we will see that science proper is the natural outflow of belief in God, however contrary that may be to popular opinion.

---

[161]   Rebecca McLaughlin, *Confronting Christianity*, p. 109

[162]   Fred Hoyle, quoted in Stephen Hawking, *Brief Answers, to the Big Questions*, 2018, p. 47–8

[163]   Steven Weinberg said, 'Over many centuries science has weakened the hold of religion, not by disproving the existence of God, but by invalidating arguments for God based on what we observe in the natural world. The multiverse idea offers and explanation of why we find our universe favourable to life that does not rely on the benevolence of a creator, and so if correct will leave still less support for religion.' Alan Lightman, *Accidental Universe*, p. 13

[164]   Richard Dawkins constantly says this.

SCIENCE IS NOT ALWAYS SCIENCE, EVEN FROM A SCIENTIST

What is science? Richard Feynman, who was awarded the 1965 Nobel Prize for his work on the development of quantum field theory, was a brilliant teacher. In one of his lectures on physics he defines for us the scientific method when trying to find a new law. He says:

> First, we guess it [audience laughter], no, don't laugh, that's the truth. Then we compute the consequences of the guess, to see . . . if this law we guess is right . . . what it would imply. And then we compare the computation results to nature, or we say compare to experiment or experience—compare it directly with observations to see if it works. If it disagrees with experiment, it's wrong. In that simple statement is the key to science. It doesn't make any difference how beautiful your guess is, it doesn't matter how smart you are who made the guess, or what his name is . . . If it disagrees with experiment, it's wrong. That's all there is to it.[165]

Observe, make a guess, experiment, results . . . that's what science is. Now, take something like gravity. We can observe it (I think I observe it more in my late thirties than I did in my twenties), we can do an experiment and we can get the results. Throw the ball in the air, record its movement, chart the parabellum arch

---

165   See: Feynman Lectures on Physics: *https://www.youtube.com/watch?v=XwzDPxo6-94*

it produces and you can measure how strong or weak the force is. That's science. However, it seems to me that certain ideas, which come under the banner of science, go far beyond this. In *Our Mathematical Universe*, Max Tegmark is very honest when he puts forward his case for a multiverse. He says:

> Is it really science to talk about such crazy things that we can't even observe, or have I crossed the line into pure philosophical speculation? ... The influential Austro-British Philosopher Karl Popper popularised the now widely accepted adage 'if it's not falsifiable, then it's not scientific' ... if a theory can't be tested even in principle, then it's logically impossible to ever falsify it, which, by Popper's definition, means that it is unscientific. It follows then that, the only thing that can have any hope of being scientific is a theory. Which brings us to a very important point: parallel universes are not a theory, but a prediction of certain theories.[166]

For Tegmark, Popper and Feynman, there is a clear-cut line between what is science and what is not science. Let's apply this and look at an often-quoted statement from Stephen Hawking describing the origin of this universe.

> Because there is a Law like gravity, the universe can and will create itself from nothing.[167]

[166] Max Tagmark, *Our Mathematical Universe*, 2015, p. 123–125
[167] Stephen Hawking & Leonard Mlodinow, *The Grand Design*, 2010, p. 180

Can you see that this is not a statement of 'science'? I am not saying that it is not based on anything at all, there is mathematical substance, but look at the surety of the statement, 'the universe *can* and *will* create itself from nothing.' This goes beyond 'observe, make a guess, experiment, results', does it not? It is a prediction, or better, a statement of philosophy—and not very good philosophy. As John Lennox points out about Professor Hawking's statement that it is very difficult to make a statement with three glaring contradictions in it.[168] Firstly, there is a law in his judgement, so he cannot say there is nothing. Secondly, 'laws' do not create anything, they describe what is happening. Thirdly, how can something create itself? It's impossible.[169] I respect Stephen Hawking, but I really cannot go here with him. This is at best a prediction, or at worst bad philosophy, but it is not science.

I am not saying we should not make predictions. No; we need prediction, we need the 'guess' that Feynman was talking about. Plus, predictions can be right, science has that logical power to it. For that's how Neptune was discovered in 1846 because of Le Verrier's prediction,[170] or that's how the 'Higgs particle' in 2012 was discovered from Peters Higgs's prediction in 1964. But we should call predictions, predictions. It is when scientists wander off into philosophy or prediction while maintaining that it is science, then I raise an eyebrow. When Rosenberg was maintaining that science is the foundation of atheism, but did not actually use science to make that judgement, did you notice that it wasn't a statement of science? In the same way, Hawking's prediction about

---

[168] John Lennox, *Can Science Explain Everything?*, 2019, p. 34–41

[169] I am tempted to add a fourth point here that I am unsure about because I am not a physicist, and I haven't read it and it seems so basic to me. I am in unchartered territory: but how can you have gravity without mass?

[170] Marcus Chown, *The Ascent of Gravity*, 2017, p. 69–74

the self-creating universe is not science proper. Again, it is not wrong to make predictions—that is part of the pursuit—but call it such. It is the assertion—that this prediction or philosophy *is* science—that I think goes beyond what science is. So does Feynman. We all agree on the ball experiment and stand in awe at the beauty of gravity in action, but when we take gravity and give it 'god-like' powers in bringing this world into existence, disagreements will happen. I am thankful to Max Tegmark for his honesty.

There is another kind of 'science-plus'. Astronomer Royal of Great Britain, Sir Martin Rees, in his book, *Our Cosmic Habitat*, gives us an amazing tour of a universe so fine-tuned that it demands an answer. What is his answer? What is his scientific explanation of the fine-tuning of our universe? He says:

> If one does not believe in providential design, but still thinks the fine-tuning needs some explanation, there is another perspective – a highly speculative one, so I should reiterate my health warning at this stage. *It is the one I much prefer* [emphasis mine], however, even though in our present state of knowledge any such preference can be no more than a hunch.[171]

He is very honest in telling us why he believes what he believes: it is his preference. Mathematics might open the door to the multiverse, but his preference pushes him in. Or take Professor Paul Davies agreeing with Hawking on the origin of the universe, when he says:

---

[171] Martin Rees, *Our Cosmic Habitat*, 2017, p. 164

There's no need to invoke anything supernatural in the origins of the universe or of life. *I have never liked the idea of divine tinkering* [emphasis mine]: for me it is much more inspiring to believe that a set of mathematical laws can be so clever as to bring all these things into being.[172]

This is not a scientific statement; this is preference, or a philosophy. It is simply what he likes.

You may now be thinking, 'Well, you are just influenced by your preference or philosophy!' and I admit that, to a degree, I must be. Throughout this book I have said that the best explanation of the universe; in its origin, fine-tuning, uniqueness and complexity, is God. The 'best' god, the one that uniquely fits, is the God of the Bible. That is me interpreting the universe and the science before me. I find it interesting that a scientist can be celebrated for making a 'prediction' or 'preference' because it is an explanation without God, but if I was to piece together a string of evidence, and then make a prediction of a Creator, I am not taken seriously.

Unfortunately, certain extreme atheistic scientists have done a good job of driving a wedge between God and science, often quoting examples of Christianity stunting scientific progress, Galileo's imprisonment by the Church being favoured among them. On the other side of the fence, certain Christian leaders have been guilty of demonising science, throwing holy water over unsuspecting scientists as they happily conduct their life. There should be room for dialogue. I love science. I love all that the pursuit of science has brought us. I love that I can sit in a warm house, that I can

---

[172] Quoted in John Lennox, *Can Science Explain Everything?*, 2019, p. 39

watch TV, that I have clean drinking water, that I can travel the world and that I can write this on my laptop. Christianity is not, nor should it be, in opposition to real science. I am not scared of what science can and will reveal. I love the new discoveries made by scientists and I pray for them, in fact our church was praying for the scientists on the front line of the fight against the coronavirus.

The war is not between God and science, but over how we interpret the data, whether that is through our philosophy of how we see the world, or the preferences we have. Our world-view is made up of a lot of different things that go beyond science; our intuition, our understanding of the universe (science) our upbringing and our experiences in life.[173] In general conversation, I have found that very few people reject belief in a God for purely intellectual reasons. It may seem that way at the start of the conversation, but often I find that they have also been influenced by a traumatic event, or a bad example of faith, or are just pushed down by guilt and rules. We don't come to conclusions in a vacuum. My point is, there is no real war between science and God, but rather between theism and atheism, or whatever view of the world you personally hold to. It is in the worldview behind the explanation of the science that the parting lines are found. Please notice this, as it is important. What we disagree about is generally not the science. Go through this book with that in mind and you will hopefully find that, scientifically, you will disagree with very little. You might, however, differ with how I interpret or explain the science.

---

[173]   David Gooding & John Lennox, *Being Truly Human*, 2018, *Series Introduction.*

The fact that God is not at war with science is borne out by the sheer number of people in the scientific community who are believers in God. In 100 *years of Nobel Prizes*, Baruch Aba Shalev says that between the years 1901 and 2000, 65.4% of Nobel prize Laureates have identified as Christian, in some form. Overall, Christians have won 78.3% of all Nobel Prizes in Peace, 72.5% in Chemistry, 65.3% in Physics, 62% in Medicine, 54% in Economics and 49.5% in Literature awards.[174] Added to these statistics, it is rightly noted that a lot of the great pioneers of science were believers in God: Roger Bacon, William of Ockham, Galileo, Kepler, Pascal, and Robert Boyle, to name just a few. Other Christian scientists include Sir Isaac Newton, famous for formulating the laws of gravity and motion; Michael Faraday, who is considered one of the best experimental scientists in history and is best known for his work on electromagnetism; and James Clerk-Maxwell who is responsible for bringing together electricity, magnetism, and light and conducted his scientific research while being an elder in a local church. The list goes on, from Lord Kelvin to Georges Lemaître—the Belgian astronomer and cosmologist who formulated the modern big-bang theory; to Gregor Mendel—a Friar who, through studying peas in the gardens of St Thomas Abby, formed the basic ideas of genetic breeding. These men who, serious about science, formed the fundamental principles of our understanding of the basic forces of the universe, were believers in God. If Rosenberg was right, then none of these people should believe in God. It should be said that the twenty-first century is no different: there continues to be many

---

[174] John Lennox, *Can Science Explain Everything?*, 2019, p. 17

believers in the scientific community[175]. Can you see that the war is not between science and God, but between atheism and religion, between naturalism and theism?

THE VOICE OF THE HISTORIANS

What really digs at the heel of this supposed war is the way the scientific method developed. Eminent Australian ancient historian Edwin Judge says:

> The modern world is the product of a revolution in scientific method . . . both experimentation in science, and the citing of sources as evidence in history, arise from the worldview of Jerusalem, not Athens, from Jews and Christians, not the Greeks.[176]

According to Judge, history shows that the scientific revolution came from the Jewish and Christian worldview. He is not alone in his estimation, as Stephen Meyer notes:

> In truth, a chorus of 20th and 21st century historians, philosophers, and sociologists of science tell a significantly different story (to what is commonly propagated). These histories note that belief in God—and Christianity specifically—played a decisive role in the rise of modern science during the 16th and 17th centuries.[177]

---

[175] *https://en.wikipedia.org/wiki/List_of_Christians_in_science_and_technology*
[176] John Lennox, *Can Science Explain Everything*, 2019, p. 20
[177] Stephen Meyer, *The Return of the God Hypothesis*, 2021, p. 19

He goes on to give a list of historians who agree with this.[178]

It is not that other empires had not made discoveries or were not technologically advanced: the Egyptians designed and built great pyramids, palaces and funerary monuments; the Chinese invented the compass, block printing and gunpowder; the Romans built great roads and aqueducts; the Greeks had great philosophers, some of whom studied nature extensively. But, as Pfunder and Lucas say, 'what we have in many cultures is technology rather than science.'[179] None of these cultures developed the scientific methods for investigating nature that arose in Eastern Europe between around 1500 and 1750 ad. Peter E. Hodgson (physicist and historian) made a similar observation:

> Many civilizations had the material requirements for the growth of science … If we think about what is needed for the viable birth of science, we see first of all that it needs a fairly well-developed society, so that some of its members can spend most of their time just thinking about the world, without the constant preoccupation of finding the next meal. It needs some simple technology, so that the apparatus required for experiments can be constructed. There must also be a system of writing, so that the results can

[178] Lindberg, *Medieval Science and Religion*; Gingerich, *God's Universe*; Hooykass, *Religion and the Rise of Modern Science*; Merton, *Science, Technology and Society in the Seventh Century England*; Duhem, *The System of World*; Russell, *The Conflict of Science and Religion*; *Cross-Currents*; Whitehead, *Science and the Modern World*; Hodgson, *The Christian Origin of Science*, *The Roots of Science and its Fruits*, *Theology and Modern Physics*; Barbour, *Religion and Science*; Kaiser, *Creation and the History of Science*; Rolston, *Science and Religion*; Fuller, *Science vs Religion*; Harrison, *The Bible, Protestantism, and the rise of Natural Science*, *The Fall of Man and the Foundations of Science*; Stark, *For the Glory of God*

[179] Pfundner and Lucas, *Think God, Think Science*, 2008, p. 6

be recorded and sent to the other scientists, and a mathematical notation for the numerical results of measurements. These may be called the material necessities of science.[180]

Many societies had 'these material requirements for the growth of science' down through the years, so why did the scientific revolution arise in Europe? It seems this was because only the Christian West had the necessary intellectual presuppositions for the rise of science. For the scientific method to arise, there needed to be an emancipation from the early Aristotelian Greek thought. Historians have found that the reaffirmation of the Judeo-Christian doctrine of creation [in the sixteenth-seventeenth centuries] has spilled over into interpreting reality,'[181] that is, our method in observation, and experimentation.

HOW THEOLOGY FUELS SCIENCE

There are aspects of the Christian mindset that seemed to help the rise of the scientific method. Firstly, *the regularity of nature*. How can Feynman make a guess, or Max Tegmark make predictions? The scientific method of guessing, then repeated experimentation and gathering of results, can only work if the world around us is regular. A belief that the world is regular comes straight out of the Biblical doctrine of creation. C. S. Lewis, summing up the work of Alfred North Whitehead, famously said, 'Men became scientific because they expected law in nature, and

---

[180] Hodgson, *The Christians Origin of Science*, quoted Stephen Meyer, *The Return of the God Hypothesis*, p. 21

[181] Pfundner and Lucas, *Think God, Think Science*, 2008, p. 5

they expected law in nature because they believed in a lawgiver.'[182] Says Stephen Meyer:

> [The doctrine of creation] shaped these early pioneers of
> the scientific method, and because of it, they expected
> its regularity. You see through their writings the theistic
> ways they have of describing this universe, it is likened
> to a book, a clock, or a law-governed realm.[183]

The obvious implication is that someone wrote the book, designed the clock and thought up the law. This should not shock us as the Bible they read constantly affirmed this regularity. For example, in Ezekiel, God says, 'I have established my covenant with day and night and the fixed laws of heaven and earth.'[184] God is speaking to the nation of Israel and points to the fixed laws of nature as a testimony of how faithful He's going to be to his people. Similarly, He speaks to Noah and makes a covenant with him, promising that nature would be regular, that there would be 'seedtime and harvest'.[185] The only reason that physics works at all is that experiments are repeatable. The only reason they're repeatable is because God is faithful in governing the universe.

The implications of this make some scientists uncomfortable. It means that in order to do science, to make predictions and guesses, you need to have a little faith: not in God, but in the regularities of this world. Adam Rutherford says, 'Science is

---

[182]   C. S. Lewis, *Miracles*, 1974
[183]   Stephen Meyer, *The Return of the God Hypothesis*, p. 30
[184]   Jerimiah 33:25
[185]   Genesis 8:22

emphatically not a belief system. It doesn't require faith . . .'[186] I don't agree and, more convincingly, neither did Einstein. He said:

> [Science] can only be created by those who are thoroughly imbued with the aspiration towards the truth and understanding. This source of feeling, however, springs from the sphere of religion. To this there also belongs the faith in the possibility that the regulations valid for the world of existence are rational, that is, comprehensible to reason. I cannot conceive a genuine man of science without that profound faith. The situation may be expressed by an image: science without religion is lame, religion without science is blind.[187]

We need to 'believe' in the regularities of nature in order to make a prediction or guess. God gives us a firm basis to do so.

Please forgive the middle-aged digression here, but I should add that the doctrine of creation also said 'go and explore'. The original mandate to Adam was to 'have dominion'[188] over the world, to go and discover those 'four rivers and the minerals at their foot'.[189] To learn how this world works and use that understanding to subdue the bad and to positively thrive. In fact, Adam was encouraged by God to compile a list of the animals around him, something we now call taxonomy. Robert Boyle, the father of modern chemistry, argued that God's freedom required an empirical and observable approach to the scientific method, that

---

[186] https://www.theguardian.com/science/2015/aug/22/can-we-trust-science-academic-journal-peer-review-retraction
[187] Quoted in John Lennox, *Can Science explain Everything*, 2019, p. 46
[188] Genesis 1:17, Genesis 2:17
[189] Genesis 2:12-14

scientists needed to look and to find out. As Ian Barber, a historian of science, explains, 'The doctrine of creation implies that the details of nature can be known only by observing them.'[190] This, it should be said, was against the flow of Greek armchair philosophy and the way it viewed the world. Creation said that the natural world is real and not an illusion, basically good and therefore worth studying. Creation said that the natural world isn't divine (unlike pantheism) and so it isn't wicked to experiment upon it. Creation said that the natural world isn't governed by multiple competing and/or capricious forces (unlike polytheism), but that it is governed by a rational order (like theism). Can you see that if science and religion were so opposed, it might well have been the case that science would never have got going?

Secondly, we need *a mind that can understand*. Since nature has been designed by the same rational mind who designed the human brain, the early modern scientist who began to investigate nature also assumed that nature was intelligible. That is, it could be understood by the human intellect. The universe, they said, was cosmos, not chaos. Philosopher Holmes Rolston III makes the point this way:

> It was monotheism that launched the coming of physical science, for it premised an intelligible world, sacred but disenchanted, a world with a blueprint, which was therefore open to the searches of the scientists. The great pioneers in physics—Newton, Galileo, Kepler,

---

[190]   Stephen Meyer, *The Return of the God Hypothesis*, 2021, p. 24

Copernicus—believed themselves called to find evidence of God in the physical world.[191]

As Kepler himself said:

> God wanted us to recognize [natural laws and that God made this possible] by creating us after his own image so that we could share in his own thoughts[192]

The doctrine of creation squarely teaches that humans uniquely are made in the image of God.[193] They have a rationale that other beings don't have. Agnostic, Steve Fuller admits that:

> While I cannot honestly say that I believe in a divine personal creator, no plausible alternative has yet been offered to justify the pursuit of science as a search for the ultimate systematic understanding of reality . . . atheism as a positive doctrine has done precious little for science.

He even argues that:

> Science . . . makes sense only if there is an overall design to nature that we are especially well-equipped to fathom, even though most of it has little bearing on our day-to-day animal survival. Humanity's creation in the image of God . . . provides the clearest historical rationale for the

[191] Rolston, *Science and Religion*, 1988, p. 39, quoted in Stephen Meyer, *The Return of the God Hypothesis*, 2021, p. 25

[192] Stephen Meyer, *The Return of the God Hypothesis*, 2021, p. 25

[193] Genesis 1:29

rather specialised expenditure of effort associated with science.[194]

Theism enables us to arrive at a position where we can genuinely and with confidence, 'Observe, make a guess, experiment, results.' Far from Christianity being in opposition to science, the voice of history tells us that out of the Judeo-Christian mindset came the modern scientific method and so the rise of the scientific revolution. It's important to let this sink in, especially in an age where we are often told believing in God makes you stupid and backward. This biblical way of thinking led to scientific discovery. As Alvin Plantinga said:

> Modern science arose within the bosom of Christian theism . . . it is a spectacular display of the image of God in us human beings.[195]

CAN WE TRUST OURSELVES?

In the film The Matrix, there is a scene where the crew of the Nebuchadnezzar are eating dinner and talking about how food tastes within the Matrix. They joke that everything tastes like chicken, doubting whether they were tasting things as they really were, or if the taste had been made up by their computer overlords. You can see how the doubt arises. If their minds are connected to and are fed by the matrix program, how could they

---

[194] Fuller, Science vs Religion?, quoted by Peter S. Williams, https://www.bethinking.org/does-science-disprove-god/is-christianity-unscientific

[195] Alvin Plantinga, Evolution and Design in James K. Beilby (ed.), For Faith and Clarity, Baker, 2006, p. 212, quoted Peter S. Williams: https://www.bethinking.org/does-science-disprove-god/is-christianity-unscientific

know what is true and false? The same type of doubt has crept in when it comes to trusting our minds for all kinds of knowledge and scientific pursuit. The problem goes like this: if this world is the product of mindless, unguided forces, just serving evolutionary development, then our minds are also a product of those forces. As David Berlinski says:

> The most unwelcome conclusion of evolutionary psychology is also the most obvious: if evolutionary psychology is true, some form of genetic determinism must be true as well. Genetic determinism is simply the thesis that the human mind is the expression of its human genes. No slippage is rationally possible.[196]

Replace 'the Matrix' with 'Unguided Force of Evolution' and you get the idea. C. S. Lewis saw this many years ago when he said:

> If the feeling of certainty which we express by words like 'must be' and 'therefore' and 'since' is a real perception of high things outside our own minds really 'must' be, well and good. But if this certainty is merely a feeling in our own minds are not a genuine insight into the realities beyond them—if it merely represents the way our minds happened to work—then we can have no knowledge. Unless human reasoning is valid no science can be true.[197]

---

[196] David Berlinski, *The Devil's Delusion*, 2009, p. 177
[197] C.S Lewis, *Miracles*, 1974, p. 21

This is a powerful argument; 'unless human reasoning is valid no science can be true.' If you thought for a minute that a computer or a car or an aeroplane was formed and controlled by unguided, mindless processes, you would never trust them to perform a function—to drive to the shop or fly to a different country. We must be able to trust that our minds are right and true. In a lecture on this subject, I was surprised to hear John Lennox cite Charles Darwin as the source of his argument. Darwin said, 'With me the horrid doubt always arises whether the conviction of man's mind, which has been developed from the mind of lower animals, is of any value or at all trustworthy.'[198]

Atheist philosopher Thomas Nagel agrees with this in his book, *Mind and Cosmos*, saying:

> Evolutionary naturalism implies that we shouldn't take any of our convictions seriously, including the scientific world picture on which evolutionary naturalism itself depends.[199]

When I read and thought through the implications of this it was startling to me. The only way I can see, to genuinely trust our minds, is if there is someone trustworthy behind them. I find it frustrating when people say that God is at war with science. But, if our minds cannot be trusted, then it is atheism that is at war with science, rather than the other way around.

[198] Letter to William Graham, 3rd July, 1881. *Darwin Correspondence Project*, goo.gl/Jfyu9Q, quoted by John Lennox, *Can Science Explain Everything?*, 2019, p. 48
[199] Thomas Nagel, *Mind and Cosmos*, 2012, p. 14

THE UNREASONABLE EFFECTIVENESS

The language of science is mathematics, and it is uniquely suited as the guarantor of objectivity and precision.[200] But why does it work so well? One of the major things that has fascinated and interested thinking mathematicians is what Wigner[201] called 'the unreasonable effectiveness' of mathematics. It is unlikely to read a book on mathematics, or listen to a mathematician talk about the cosmos, without them referring at some point to this paper by Wigner. How does an equation in the mind of a man have a real time application? Take Einstein's time clocks, where he postulates that two people moving at different speeds will experience time differently. It is interesting to think about, but how does that have a bearing on my life? Well, because of this I can find my way through the highways and byways to find my destination through satellite navigation. Take a moment to contemplate Newton's original equations of gravity; through them we now know what force is needed to break gravity and get the satellites up there in the first place. Then there is Alan Turing's work in computation to build the processing power for real time calculations. You get the point. The more you start to think about it, the more we agree with Galileo that 'the book of nature is written in the language of mathematics.'

---

[200] Paul Davies, *The Language of God*, 1992, p. 93

[201] Eugene Wigner (1902–1995) worked on the Manhattan Project, after which he hired as the Director of Research and Development at the Clinton Laboratory (now the Oak Ridge National Laboratory). In 1960, he received the Nobel Prize in Physics for contributions to Theory of the atomic nucleus and the elementary particles, particularly through the discovery and application of fundamental symmetry principles.

For some of us, the word 'mathematics', transports us back to our teens, sitting in a classroom as our eyes start to glaze over. You may want to stop reading now, or even feel like sticking your finger in your eye for ever letting the word 'mathematics' in through the eye gate. Maybe I have gone too far, but if maths is not your thing, press on, you are nearly there. Words like arithmetic, algebra, calculus, trigonometry and geometry will not help. But take trigonometry, which studies the relationship between sides and angles in triangles. Over 2,200 years ago, Aristarchus of Samos, by measuring the angle of a 'half-moon' to the sun and working out an angle of 87 degrees, made a brilliant attempt to guess the distance to our sun.[202] Now think about that for one minute, a formula, in the head of a person, worked in reality to measure a distance. Mathematics works in reality.

We need to take a step sideways for a second, to consider the fact that mathematics is not physical. There is something about it that is elusive to us. The Peugeot car company began as a small family business but today it employs about 200,000 people worldwide and produces more than 1.5 million automobiles, earning revenues of about €55 billion. In what sense can we say that the company Peugeot exists? There are many Peugeot vehicles, but these are not the company. Even if every Peugeot car in the world was simultaneously junked and sold for scrap metal, the Peugeot company would not disappear. Peugeot is a figment of our collective imagination. Lawyers call this a 'legal fiction'. It can't be pointed at, and it is not a physical object, but it exists.[203] It is

---

[202] Max Tegmark, *Our Mathematical Universe*, 2015, p. 23: The angle turned out to be 89.85, making the sun twenty times further away than he thought and was worked out 1,500 year later by Copernicus, when he was thinking about the size and shape of our solar system.

[203] Yuval Noah Harari, *Sapiens*, 2011, p. 31–32

ethereal yet it interacts with the real world. The same can be said of mathematics. Heinrich Hertz, the first to produce and detect radio waves in the laboratory, once said, 'One cannot escape the feeling that these mathematical formulas have an independent existence of their own . . . .'[204] Nobel prize winning mathematician, Roger Penrose, believes that mathematics has an independent existence, a 'Platonic existence' he calls it, 'that is radically distinct from physical space and time.' He says:

> [Certainly] mathematicians view mathematics as something out there, which seems to have a reality independent of the ordinary kind of reality of things like chairs, which we normally think of as real.[205]

How is it that with a few symbols on a page you can describe a wealth of physical phenomena? While being interviewed on *Closer to Truth*, Penrose said:

> People often find it puzzling that something abstract like mathematics could really describe reality. But you cannot understand atomic particles and structures, such as gluons and electrons except with mathematics.

It is amazing to consider the successes that have been achieved. Wigner in, *The Unreasonable Effectiveness of Mathematics*, notes the sheer breadth of utility of mathematics. You always get more out than you put in. Think of all the discoveries that

---

[204] Quoted Paul Davies, *The Mind of God*, 1992, p. 145
[205] Interview on *Closer to Truth*.

have come from Newton's original discovery.[206] Mathematics not only describes the breadth of this world, but also its exactness. Einstein remarked, 'How can it be that mathematics, being after all a product of human thought which is independent of experience, is so admirably appropriate to the objects of reality?' I find it interesting that Wigner sums up his argument by saying:

> The enormous usefulness of mathematics in the natural sciences is *something bordering on the mysterious* [emphasis mine] and that there is no rational explanation for it.

Notice that it borders on the mysterious. For him, the miracle of the appropriateness of the language of mathematics for the formulation of the laws is super-rational. For the believer in God, the intelligibility of the universe and the effectiveness of mathematics are perfectly reasonable. God is an intelligent Creator who's responsible for both the universe and the human mind. He indeed 'is a mathematician'.[207]

TIME FOR TEA

One of my favourite chemical reactions is making a cup of tea. I say chemical reaction, but it is really a mere mixing. Nothing massively changes, other than the water leaching the tea by the process of diffusion. The point is, the two exist side by side,

---

[206] Alan Lightman, *An Accidental Universe*, p. 8
[207] James Jeans, quoted by Paul Davies, *The Mind of God*, 1992, p. 14

making a wonderful product that produces joy. A far cry from potassium and water.

One of the most scientific symbols in the city of Armagh, where I live, is the observatory. Interestingly, it was opened and heavily funded by a religious man, Archbishop Robinson. He did this with the Reverend J. A. Hamilton, who had his own small private observatory in Cookstown and wanted an opportunity to discover more of the universe.[208] Both men were deeply religious, but also deeply committed to exploring this world. 'Science and religion,' says Professor Sir John Polkinghorne, '. . . are friends, not foes, in the common quest for knowledge. Some people may find this surprising, for there's a feeling throughout our society that religious belief is outmoded, or downright impossible, in a scientific age. I don't agree. In fact, I'd go so far as to say that if people in this so called 'scientific age' knew a bit more about science than many of them actually do, that they'd find it easier to share my view.'[209]

To truly understand what science is will show us that the war is not 'Science vs God'. The history of Christianity laid the foundation for science and theology gives it a basis, for we have a regular world and a mind to understand it. The Christian view is that, like Adam, we are to go and discover, and with science to understand this world as friends, not foes. I wonder what 'Mr Science and Reason' thinks of this?

---

[208] Armagh Observatory and Planetarium website: *https://www.armagh.space/ heritage/armagh-observatory/history/an-observatory-for-armagh*

[209] John Polkinghorne, *Quarks, Chaos and Christianity*, 1994, quoted in, Lee Strobel, *The Case for the Creator*, 2004, p. 69

CHAPTER 7

CHRISTIANITY'S ORIGIN STORY

If you are still with me at this point, I am delighted: this is the chapter I really want you to read. Since we are going to look at Christianity's origin story, it might be good to break from reading this and go to Appendix 1, where I have included the text of the first chapter of Genesis. I am amazed by the number of people who have strong views on what Genesis 1 means, or what they have heard it means, but have never read it or engaged with it for themselves. Before we go any further, may I encourage you to grab a cup of tea or coffee and take a few minutes to read through it now?

At times we can all be very good at spotting problems but having no answers. I admire people who not only see the difficulties but also come up with genuine solutions. There is a man in our church who has this skill; he not only sees problems but also the possible ways of fixing them. He's a great guy to have around. Christianity is not the grumpy old man in the corner, always ready to point out what is wrong with the world, but never rolling up his sleeves to give positive answers. Instead, it offers a response: an origin story that helps us navigate our beginnings. Let's look at that now.

WHAT THIS 'ORIGIN STORY' IS DOING

Genesis 1[210] is probably one of the most famous pieces of literature in the world. Endless books have been written about it, speeches have quoted from it and films have narrated it. It was even read from space by the crew of Apollo 8. It has been called 'Mystery and Majesty'[211] and it is not hard to see why. The first phrase, 'In the beginning God created the heavens and earth', is somehow both piercing and awe-inspiring. It is concise, just eleven words in English, but pregnant with a thousand embryos of thought.[212] This is an amazing piece of literature but how do we understand it?

Let's start by thinking about the book of Genesis itself. Customarily believed to be written or compiled by Moses,[213] Genesis means 'origin' or 'beginning', and that is what it seems to be about. Genesis tells us about the origins of the universe itself: of humanity, culture, beauty, work, agriculture, science and relationships; of the problems and sufferings of this world; of language; and of the beginning of the Hebrew nation itself. In that sense it is a 'history'.

If you read through Genesis, you will see very quickly what many scholars and commentators have noted; the phrase, 'these are the generations of', or 'these are the HISTORIES of' runs

---

[210] The first section is Genesis 1:1–2:3, but I will call this 'Genesis 1' for convenance.

[211] Atkinson, *The Message of Genesis*, 1990, p. 13

[212] I am honestly not sure where I got this turn of phrase from. I suspect I have read it but I cannot remember where.

[213] My intention in this chapter is not to enter this debate, but to let the text of Genesis one speak on its own merit. If you want to read the debates and difficulties over the date, authorship etc. please read Kitchen, Wenham, Hamilton. There you will get all you need. My own position is that Moses' authorship or compilation is authentically accurate, not just because the weight of scholarship points that way, but also because Jesus Christ himself authenticates it.

through the book. These 'toledots', as they are known, are an ancient literary technique that 'form section headings and divides.'[214] They occur ten times[215] throughout the book, introducing us to a certain level of history and focusing our view on a person, or a particular line and genealogy. I remember sitting in a Bible study with Professor David Gooding, who was an amazing Bible teacher and classics scholar. He showed us how this phrase not only runs through the book but also helps us navigate it. When you lay the occurrences of these 'toledots' out in order, it can look like this:[216]

1:1–2:3	The Creation of Order.
2:4–4:26	The Creation of Mankind.
5:1–9:29	The Judgement and Start of a New World
10:1–25:11	The Creation of a New Order
25:12–35:29	The Creation of a New Man
36:1–50:26	The Judgement and Start of a New World

A lot of these sections would need explanation,[217] but I want you to firstly notice *when* the recording of history starts. The first statement of 'histories' is at 2:4.[218] This means that the first creation account of Genesis 1:1–2:3, stands outside the recounting of history proper. I emphasise this because of its importance. The first mention of the phrase 'these are the generations of', the

---

[214] C. John Collins, *Genesis 1-4: A Linguistic, Literary, and Theological Commentary*, 2006

[215] Genesis 2:4, 5:1, 6:9, 10:1, 11:10, 10:27, 25:12, 25:19, 36:1, and finally in 37:2.

[216] If you notice the symmetry in the sections, it is an impressive feat.

[217] See David Gooding's exposition: *https://www.myrtlefieldhouse.com/genesis*

[218] Some take this toledot as a sum statement of Genesis 1:1–2:3. If so, this would be the only toledot that it functions in such a way, since all other references act as 'starting divisions'.

toledot that forms the structural division of the book that tells us that Genesis is a historical book is at 2:4, standing outside the first creation story.

Secondly, and seemingly counter to what I have just said, when you start reading the text you see that it reads as a historical narrative. It is very 'Earthy' in that the contents are not mystical. There are no magical creatures, strange lands and strange incantations; instead, we encounter the 'normal' things we see around us: the sky, sea, trees, fish, birds, animals, and humans. It is a story: a narrative in that sense. Genesis was originally written in Hebrew, not English, and so a lot of scholars refer to the way in which the original Hebrew is written,[219] identifying this passage as narrative. It is historical in that it points to something that is happening in the text and has happened at a point in history. That is my very opposite second step.

Thirdly then, as you continue to read through Genesis 1, you will start to notice that this first chapter contains something more than just history, a kind of 'history-plus'. Take verse 1 which says, 'In the beginning God created the heavens and earth'. I don't know how else to interpret this, other than to conclude that there was a point when God 'created'[220] everything: as the Nicene Creed puts it, 'all that is seen and unseen'. This is what is meant by 'heavens and earth'—the extreme ends and everything in between. So, verse 1 is an actual event. In that sense it is history. Verse two says; 'the Earth was without form and void'. The Hebrew words for without form (*tohu*), and void (*bohu*), rhyme. This might

---

[219] The Hebrew tense signifies a narrative, see C. John Collins, Genesis 1–4, 2006, p. 43

[220] The Hebrew word 'bara' is always used of God's creative acts (Isa 40:26, 45:7, 8). The New Testement envisages (Heb 11:3, John 1:1-3) that creation 'ex-nihilo' is in view here. Creation out of nothing.

Day 1	Day 4
'And God says'	'And God says'
Light	Sun, Moon and Stars (Lights)
'Separates Light from Darkness'	'Separate the Day from the Night'

Day 2	Day 5
'And God says'	'And God says'
Expanse (sky)	Birds
Water below (sea)	Fish

Day 3	Day 6
And God says'	'And God says'
Land and Seas	Animal Life
'And God says'	'And God says'
Biological Life	Human Life

Day 7—God rests from his creation work

Table 1

seem insignificant, but the rest of the chapter is highly structured and turns on these two words. It flows like this: verses 1 and 2 stand apart as an introduction and a first move of God to create this universe; then in response to this Earth being 'without form and void' you have six days, all beginning with 'And God said'. On the first three days, he answers 'tohu' and he shapes and forms the world. Then, in the last three days, he fills the *bohu* in this world. Then you have the rest day, the Sabbath. When you lay the 'work-days' in their threes side by side, you see significant, obvious symmetry. On day one light comes to be and on day four the lights are appointed. In both days, light in some form is being separated from darkness. On day two, the waters and the 'heavens', that is the sky and the seas, are formed. On day five these areas are filled by the creation of sea creatures and birds. On day three the land is made, but then God speaks a second time to create biological life, in trees and plants. On day six God creates animals to fill the land, then He speaks a second time to create humans. He forms this Earth in the first three days, and then He fills what he shapes in the last three (see *Table* 1 on the previous page).

Do you see the *symmetry* when laid out like this? You could hardly miss it. This is carefully ordered, meticulously structured and based on the rhyme of *tohu* and *bohu*. Added to this, the whole chapter is a literary marvel, full of devices used to make its point. You cannot help but notice its *repetition*: 'The evening and the morning nth day'; 'And God said'; 'it was good'; 'according to their kinds' etc. Then there is the emphasis on *numbers*, something the Hebrew reader would see very quickly but is less obvious in our English translations. They particularly revolve around the number seven, which is seen as the number of completion and perfection. There are seven days. The words 'God', 'expanse' (heaven), and 'Earth' are all repeated in multiples of seven. 'God' occurs thirty-five times and 'heaven and earth' twenty-one times. In addition to this, the first verse has seven Hebrew words, the second fourteen and the concluding paragraph 2:1–3 has three sentences, all containing seven words, making twenty-one words, with the middle phrase being 'the seventh day'.

This obvious symmetry, repetition and play on numbers is 'history-plus'. The text is doing something other than just recounting history to us. This has led some to say that Genesis 1 is a 'creation poem', or that this is figurative for God building His 'cosmic temple'[221] to dwell with us on Earth. I am not sure I am satisfied with this. There is certainly poetry here, but there is also that 'history' which stands outside of history proper. It is doing something, but this history is being told in imagery, repetition, and symmetry. Some have called this 'elevated prose'. It is history with literary device. It is poetry but also prose. It is not a myth, but an origin story in the real sense. Notice that, while the Genesis account is telling us about *what* happened, it is not telling us every detail of *how* it happened. Rather than just recounting the history, or the 'how' of our origins, it is telling the 'why', and it is doing so through device. The emphasis is on *why* this universe was created and, for most people, that is a bigger question.

The 'how' question and the 'why' question ask for different levels of explanation. If you were driving through the centre of town and I asked, 'How do those lights at the side of the road work?', you might start to tell me about resisters and transistors, about the flow of electricity, about photons and the frequencies of light that make green, amber and red. All of this is helpful in explaining *how* the lights work. But if I asked you, 'Why is that light there?', you would talk about other cars on the road and the need for us to stop and let the others through. You need to know the why but not necessarily the how. Both levels of explanation are there in Genesis 1, but it is WHY heavy. The language used, the structure, the climax of day six, the rest on day seven: none of that is needed if you are just dealing with the HOW.

---

[221] John Walton, *The Lost World of Genesis One*, 2009

Let's bring this together. There are four big philosophical questions that most people will ask at some point in their life: 'Where do I come from?', 'What is Life?', 'What am I?' and 'Where am I going?'. Genesis 1:1–2:3 answers the first question. This is Christianity's origin story, making sense of *our* universe through an account that is Earth-centred. Although it speaks about the universe, it addresses *us*, beginning with what we recognise and trust and know to be true. Again, there are no mythical beasts or stories; nothing is foreign to what we know, in that sense. Anything supernatural comes from a God who has no rivals, who is in control and who, uniquely, has an immense interest in humanity. This is someone we can trust. The creation story breeds a natural confidence in us, bringing us to domains we know: Earth, seas, sky, heavens (from our view), with the division of animals, birds, fish and humans into their appropriate domains. It begins by addressing humans by what is both familiar and first for us. I want you to see that this initial intuitive trust of the text is right. It is an origin story for every time and era, that makes sense of our world and is true to the things we know.

THE ANCIENT MIND

If you had read this origin story back in the ancient pagan world, what would you have thought? The discovery of some ancient creation 'myths' have helped us get some idea of what people believed then. In the exclusively polytheistic cultures of the ancient world, it would have been striking that this origin story has one God. The fact that one God is the sole Creator of everything, even of those 'things' the ancients would have deified,

144

is unique to Genesis. This idea would cut across all the ancient Eastern ideas of origins.

In the Genesis account, some of Moses' descriptions would have raised an ancient eyebrow. Instead of mentioning the names of the sun and moon, he talks about 'the greater and lesser lamps'. The most likely reason for this is the similarity between the Hebrew words for the sun and moon and the names of the Gods they deified. In effect, Moses is saying, 'They are not God's, just lamps, fashioned and appointed by the one true God.' They have no life of their own. They, like all of us, are dependent on this one true God for life. You will see that the sun is 'purposefully demoted',[222] as there is 'light' (in some form) on day one before the sun's appointment on day four. These 'lamps' are not worthy of worship: He is. They are set and appointed[223] to serve us for 'signs and for seasons',[224] not for us to worship and serve them. Take the phrase, 'and the stars' in verse 16. The stars would, to some ancient minds, be both deities and ancestors to pray to and appease. Genesis says that the stars are not controlling human destiny, the one true God is. He made them, He is over them.

Then there is the Hebrew word *bara* which means 'create'.[225] It is always used of God's creative acts[226] and it highlights His special activity in creation. *Bara* first occurs in Genesis 1:1 to describe the origin of this universe, then it is not used until verse 21, where the sea creatures are made. In verse 27, when mankind is created, it

[222] Leon Kass, *The Beginning of Wisdom*, 2006, p. 31
[223] ESV *margin*: this is probably a better rendering that the customarily 'made'. God sets them in place, Moses sees this.
[224] Genesis 1:14
[225] Different from the word 'made', *asa*. There is a major difference between 'creation' and 'making'.
[226] Isaiah 40:26, 45:7-8

appears three times. Lastly, it appears in 2:3, speaking again of the universe. On one level, the writer seems to be drawing attention to the order and levels of creation; from inanimate material to organic life, to complex life and then to humanity (we will return to this point later). But on a more superficial level that would have been noticed by an ancient world, the sea creatures are highlighted. Why? In some of the creation myths, the sea creatures (dragons) are rivals who are conquered by the Canaanite gods.[227] Here, they are not opposing gods but created creatures.

The stark contrast between this and other origin stories has led scholars to believe that Genesis 1 was written as a direct, cutting alternative to these myth stories with that direct purpose in mind. There are very loose connections[228] between some of the words used in Genesis and those used in some of the myths, but I don't think this is significant justification for making it the *main* point of Genesis 1. It is simply a consequence of truth. Look again at the opening statement, 'In the beginning God created the heaven and the earth.' While most of the myths are cosmogonies (that is, gods are part of the order), this is a straight, positive statement. The God of Genesis stands apart from this universe: He is outside it, transcendent and above it. So, although it pushes back against the false notions of the ancient day, this is not the major intent. It is not written chiefly as a polemic, but the positive truths it is teaching mean it has that effect. As Kidner says, 'this creation story has stood as a bulwark against a successive of fashionable errors—polytheism, dualism, the eternity of matter, the evil of matter and astrology,' and it does this positively. This

---

[227] Derek Kidner, *Word Biblical Commentary, Vol 1: Genesis 1-15*, 2008, p. 9
[228] Some of the words used in Genesis are vaguely similar.

is a testimony to the fact that this text speaks to all generations in all eras, getting across its message of the origins of life. Leon Kass sums this up:

> The controversial note is heard indirectly, as it were, through the deliberate, quiet utterances of scripture, which sets the opposing views at naught by silence or by subtle hint.[229]

I would add that old ideas don't tend to go away but are often rehashed. As the preacher in the book of Ecclesiastes tells us, 'There is nothing new under the sun.'[230] There are old philosophies that are reincarnating themselves in our modern world, telling us that God is in the flower, in the Earth, wind, sea and sky; that God is part of this cosmos. We need to listen to the Genesis origin story.

THE MODERN MAN—OUR FOUR QUESTIONS

Throughout this book, we have looked at four areas that seem to form some of the limits of what science can tell us. Firstly, what started everything off, how can something come from nothing? Then we asked, why is everything so fine-tuned? Next, we saw our privileged planet and asked, why Earth is so unique in the universe. Finally, we thought about the complex cell and asked, how did life and complex life come from non-life? I am not suggesting that Moses knew about the atom, gravity, elements or DNA and the intricacies of life, and yet this text, originally

---

[229] Umberto Cassuto quoted in Leon Kass, *The Beginning of Wisdom*, 2006, p. 27
[230] Ecclesiastes 1:9

written for its day, positively tells us the origins of this universe. Like it did for the ancient mind, it can do for us today. Genesis still has a defining power of what is right and wrong. So, I really believe it can also speak to our generation.

Referring to the question, 'Why is there something rather than nothing?', you will remember that Martin Heidegger said, 'That is the question . . . the first of all questions.' How did we get here? What started that initial surge of energy? Where does this matter or space or time come from? What was there 'just before' the start of things? These are the questions that keep us up at night. Recently I got into a conversation in a coffee shop with a man who, it turned out, was about to deliver a lecture on black holes at the local planetarium. My friend asked him what he thought was before the Big Bang. He replied that he didn't know and that there is no way through science that we could know. This is true and it is a limit of science. The assumption of atheism is that this physical world is all there is and, if there is no matter before the Big Bang, then there is nothing to study. So, scientifically, asking what came before the Big Bang is like asking, 'What is north of the north pole?'[231] It is 'futile.'[232] To me, looking for a source within the system sounds a bit like the ancient cosmogonies.

We have been making the point that, according to this origin story, God is not *part* of this universe, but *above it* and *before it*.[233] Surely, we can see that there is an absolute need for this kind of input. Something cannot come from nothing; something cannot come out of nothing. Genesis tells us that 'In the beginning God

---

[231] Stephen Hawking, A *Brief History Of Time*, 2009, p. 161

[232] Paul Davies, *The Goldilocks Enigma*, 2007, p. 92

[233] This is not technically a correct statement for 'time' was created alone with the universe, so you cant have a 'before' time.

created the heavens and the earth.' That God, who stands apart from this world, creates this world 'out of nothing'—a world 'not made of things that are visible'[234] and tangible. This must be a *unique* event beyond the reach of scientific instruments. Paul Davies says, 'either the cosmic origin is a natural event, or it is a supernatural event,'[235] meaning that a creation event would be a one-off supernatural event, an incident that has no complete explanation from within science and one that is not repeatable. He is not referring to God, he is not a believer in God. He means a singularity event that goes beyond nature and the natural order of things. A super-nature event in that sense. If creation was a natural, repeatable event, we would see it happening again and again. It was either natural or supernatural; these are the alternatives. The scientific community as a whole, not just Professor Davies, will talk about the start of things as a singularity. A point in 'time' in which the laws of physics, and everything known, break down. This is the very thing Genesis is emphasising: that this is unusual; that God is creating, not making but creating. It's important to grasp the difference. *Creation* comes 'out of nothing'; something new is inputted into the system. *Making*, on the other hand, uses materials already present. This is outside the realm of physics as, again, if this was an event within the normal laws of physics, why just once, why not again? Should it not be repeatable? John Leslie said, 'It would be exceedingly odd if the physical process behind the creation event bore the label "THIS MECHANISM OPERATED ONLY ONCE".'[236] His point is that if this

---

[234] Hebrews 11:3

[235] Paul Davies, *The Goldilocks Enigma*, 2007, p. 92

[236] John Leslie, *Universes*, 1989, p. 95 quoted in Davies, *The Goldilocks Enigma*, 2007, p. 93

event came from within the natural order, it should repeat and would be strange to happen just once. This start is not natural, it is supernatural. It is God creating in a one-off process. Genesis will tell us something sensible, something different from cosmogonies: there is a God who is not part of this universe, but above it, before it and beyond it. In creation He has injected energy into it, giving us the 'ultimate free-gift' of life itself. Creating time ('in the beginning'), creating space ('the heavens') and creating matter ('the Earth'). I think this is more reasonable than this universe appearing through Hawking's 'law of gravity' or Krauss's 'nothing'. Can you see how this text answers our question? There is something that stands outside of this world, with enough power, wisdom and will to create.

This is where I will go beyond the 'natural evidence' of the sciences to the level of revelation and history. There was nothing physical to study before the start and so, as we cannot study what is not there, we must go beyond physics and cosmology. It is the Christian claim that we can know what is behind creation because God has chosen to reveal Himself and tell us. The Bible is the record of God's intervening in history and the revealing who of He is. This origin story was given to Moses (on some level) by God and teaches us that there is something behind this universe. But, to a greater degree, the ultimate evidence for believing there was something before this creation, something more than this material universe, is Jesus Christ. The apostle John said, 'In the beginning was the Word' (John 1:1–14). He is referring to Jesus Christ, here called 'the Word', who was with the Father, and 'through whom all things came to be'. Jesus then 'became flesh', stepping into human history and becoming a human. God has come into this world to tell us what is true about creation, to tell us what is beyond our microscopes and experiments. Do you see that? I don't think people take the historical fact of Jesus seriously enough. No matter what recent popular atheists say, there is no real doubt amongst scholars that Jesus Christ appeared in history. Bart Ehrman, a renowned historical scholar and an outspoken agnostic, recently addressed a room of atheists about the historicity of Jesus. He said:

> This is not even an issue for scholars of antiquity . . . the reason for thinking Jesus existed is because he is abundantly attested to in the early sources . . . if you want to go where the evidence goes, I think that atheists have done themselves a disservice by jumping on the bandwagon of mysticism, because frankly, it makes you look foolish to the outside world. If that's what you're going to believe, you just look foolish.[237]

It is foolish to say that Jesus did not exist in history, in fact Ehrman says He is 'abundantly attested to in the early sources.' He might disagree with who Jesus is but not that He existed. In his book *Dominion: The Making of the Western Mind*, Tom Holland, an author and historian who is not a believer in God, says:

> The four earliest accounts of his [Jesus] execution, [that were] written some decades after his death . . . [said] there is no reason to doubt the essentials of this narrative.

---

[237]   *https://www.youtube.com/watch?v=43mDuIN5-ww*

Even the most sceptical historians have tended to accept them.[238]

What I am saying is that the historical existence of Jesus is not in doubt and that the New Testament that records His life, death, burial and resurrection is reliable. C. S. Lewis, an expert in English literature, said:

> I have been reading poems, romances, vision literature, legends and myths all my life. I know what they are like. I know none of them are like this . . . this is reportage.[239]

To read *Jesus and the Eyewitnesses* by Richard Bauckhum, or *The Historical Reliability of the New Testament* by Craig Blomberg, is to walk away believing Jesus has historically come into this world. He came that he might show us what is right and true, that he might give us an answer to our deepest questions. On that basis, it is not arrogance to give an answer to what is beyond this universe, that is just responding to what has been said to Moses and by Jesus Himself. Could it be arrogance, however, to completely rule out God as an answer, based on blind personal belief and preference?

Our second question centred around the fine-tuning of this universe. We have already established that the fine-tuning of the universe is nothing short of miraculous, and that the surprising precision of nature's physical constants makes complex life possible. We must take this seriously. Even the late Christopher

---

[238] Tom Holland, *Dominion*, 2019, p. xvii
[239] Quoted Tim Keller, *The Reason for God*, 2008, p. 106

Hitchens said, 'Not to be impressed by the fact that we are here rather than not here, is to be too easily unimpressed.'[240] We cannot just say 'it is what it is'; the odds are too great and it demands an answer. Add to this our *privileged planet*: the fact that we are in the right size and type of galaxy, at the right point in time and in the exact position in a galaxy conducive to life. We have the right host star. Our sun is the right size. It has the right type of light. Its age and distance from us are quite perfect. We have giant outer planets, like cosmic bouncers that protect us from planet killing projectiles. We have a moon that is big enough and near enough to give us stability, maintain tidal control, and keep our tilt stable. Our Earth's atmosphere is uniquely able to maintain a heat balance, but filter harmful UV rays, and it is oxygen rich and maintained by a specific carbon cycle. We have life's basic solvent, water, in abundance, together with its basic element, carbon. The core of our planet is a molten furnace that gives us continents, stabilises sea levels, creates global biodiversity, provides a global thermostat, and produces a magnetic field to guard off harmful cosmic rays. The level of fine-tuning in our universe and planet points to something.

This origin story is one reason why Christians are not deists. God is not an unenthusiastic Father who is disinterested and not involved: He is present and involved with this world. One of the striking things about Genesis 1 is that God does not create in one movement. Creation is by a process; day one, two, three, four, five, and day six of God's involvement. Here is the Fine-Tuner active and working hands-on in the creation of this planet, the seas, the sky, the Earth, and the solar system. God, presented

---

[240] https://www.youtube.com/watch?v=YL3wwlh5KS0&list=WL

in Genesis, is actively involved to produce a planet for the great climax of human life. Here, the astronomical odds of a fine-tuned universe and a privileged planet come within the grasp of his creative genius and power. He is the best explanation of the odds.

Next, we come back to the *complex cell*. How does life begin? According to geneticist Michael Denton, the break between the non-living world and the living world:

> Represents the most dramatic and fundamental of all the discontinuities of nature. Between a living cell and the most highly ordered known systems, such as a crystal or snowflake, there is a chasm as vast and absolute as it is possible to conceive.[241]

John Horgan one of America's leading scientific journalists, who identifies himself as a 'lapsed Catholic', said in 2002 that scientists have no idea how the universe was created or how:

> Inanimate matter on our little planet coalesced into living creatures . . . science, you might say, has discovered that our existence is infinitely improbable, and hence a miracle.[242]

These are men at the top of this field, talking about the 'miracle' needed to make the jump between non-life and life. Genesis is remarkable because it raises this very problem by, first, telling

---

[241] Denton, *Evolution: Still a Theory in Crisis*, 1986, p. 249–50
[242] John Horgan, *A Holiday Made for Believing*, New York Times, December 25th, 2002, quote in Stephen Meyer, *Signature in the Cell*, 2009, p. 42

us how God creates through His Word and, second, strategically emphasising the frequency of His speech.

Firstly then, God creates through His Word; each day of the creation story starts with the words 'And God said'. The idea of God creating through his Word is repeated in the rest of the Bible[243] but, when we get to the New Testament, we see that God's Word is a person. Again, John tells us, 'In the beginning was the Word . . . all things were made through him.' God's Word has the power and agency to act and create, because God's Word is Jesus Christ. He not only fully reveals God, because that's what words do, but He has the infinite resources of heaven, to create, shape, form and fill this universe.

This is a very key point when thinking about the complex cell on a very elementary level. When someone speaks, they impart 'information'. If I were to start speaking about oranges, your mind will start thinking about oranges. I am putting new information into the system. When we looked at the complex cell, we saw that at the heart of every living thing is information, the longest word ever written in four letters: T, A, G, and C; a code that determines life itself: DNA. This is no accident, is it? Again, I am not saying Moses knew about DNA but the positive truth and ideas of Genesis 1 speak to us even today.

Secondly, notice the frequency of God's speeches through Genesis 1. On days one and two, 'And God said' occurs once, but notice that God speaks twice on day three. On days four and five, God speaks once but multiple times on day six. There must be something important about days three and six, and there is. For on these days God creates different levels of 'life'. He speaks

---

[243] Psalms 33:6, Hebrews 11:3

once on day three to gather the seas and to produce land, but a second time to bring about organic life. That is deliberate from the writer, telling us that 'And God said' is what stands between non-life and life. Think of the dramatic difference between life and non-life, between that micro city of a cell we thought about in Chapter 4 and a rock at the side of a road. The chasm between life and non-life needs a further injection of information into the system, it needs God's speech. Do you see that? What Genesis is saying? It is answering the question: *Where does life come from?* The answer is from God Himself. Speaking about the need for involvement in the process of life's origin, Anthony Latham bemoans some overreaching assumptions of the making of the first complex cell, saying:

> I marvel however at how some scientists view these facts of the chemical ingredients of life being present, as if the whole problem is almost dealt with. It is true that the ingredients existed. It is also true that the ingredients to make a Rolls Royce car can be found lying on the scrapheap. I do not then jump to the conclusion that a Rolls Royce will somehow appear out of the heap without a fair amount of help from an engineer.[244]

Just because some of the ingredients are there that doesn't automatically make a cake. We need 'and God said', God's involvement. Here we have the divine Engineer, active and involved, speaking and creating, bringing this world into being and bridging that vast chasm between non-life and life. Can you see how Genesis 1

[244] Anthony Latham, *The Naked Emperor*, 2005, p. 15

is answering our questions? This origin story just makes sense. It has that ring of truth about it with which we can resonate.

A FEW THINGS TO MENTION

Just before we leave the *how*, I need to say a couple of things. Firstly, I want to emphasise something we said earlier that comes from the seventh day of creation. There is a difference between the creation and the maintenance of this universe, between the initial event and the upkeep of the normal processes of this world. Earlier we spoke of a 'singularity' where all the laws of nature break down and that is a helpful way of thinking about our origins. This was a special creation, a one off 'week', done in stages where God supernaturally broke into our world and formed and fashioned it. We should not expect this kind of event to happen today[245] in the regularities of nature because of the seventh day, or the Sabbath as it is called. Notice that on day seven God stops His 'work in *creation*'. He stops creating . . . stops doing the supernatural on this level. Therefore, I think there are certain things we will not be able to sort out through science. Not that we shouldn't try. God has not put any 'no trespassing' signs here, so we should pursue it as far as we can. This is not 'god of the gaps' thinking, that God has done it so we stop investigating it. No! This is taking seriously a Creator creating, then resting and now maintaining.

Secondly, how are we to think about the 'week' and the 'days'? To be clear, this is *my* thinking; you may or may not agree with

[245] This is not to say that God cannot break into this order and do miracles. He can, it is His right and ability, and He has. The Bible records many occasions where miracles are performed. But in this level of creative activity, creation out of nothing!

me on this. The text refers to days; it's not clear what level this is on, but they are actual times. There is the initial creation event in verse 1 then, on six occasions that we are told of, God intervenes supernaturally to shape and form this planet. The way the days are written in Hebrew doesn't mean it has to be seven straight days in a row—it is more like a diary entry: day one, two, three, four, five. The definition of 'the' sixth day and 'the' seventh day indicates that there was a definite conclusion to these creative acts. While this chapter is all about God's creative acts, we are not told what happens in the aeons in-between. At different points God intervenes, inputs information into the system and pushes the process on to its grand conclusion.

Lastly, if this is written by Moses, where did he get his information? I think this is a question few people address. After the exodus, God brought His people to Mount Sinai to give them His Law and, at that point, Moses went up the mountain to be with God. My view is that, on the mountain, Moses got visionary 'snapshots' of God's activity in six movements. That would explain why everything is from the viewpoint of Earth, and why he doesn't see the sun, moon or stars until day four, when they are not made but 'appointed'. Apparently, the early planet's atmosphere would have been a haze[246] that blanketed Earth. Some think it was like what we see in one of Saturn's moons, Titan;[247] this would mean it would not have been clear enough to see into the heavens until

---

[246] Sarah M. Hörst et al., 'Exploring the Atmosphere of Neoproterozoic Earth: The Effect of O2 on Haze Formation and Composition', *Astrophysical Journal*, 858 (May 2018): https://doi:10.3847/1538-4357/aabd7d.

[247] 'Organic Haze on Titan and the Early Earth' (Nov 28th 2006), Melissa G. Trainer, Alexander A. Pavlov, H. Langley DeWitt, Jose L. Jimenez, Christopher P. McKay, Owen B. Toon, and Margaret A. Tolbert, *https://www.pnas.org/doi/10.1073/pnas.0608561103*

the abundance of oxygen that comes on day three.[248] That's why the language is historical, in that the progression of the days is chronological, but also a vision-like snapshot. This would fit with how God begins and ends the Bible with Moses and John, Genesis and Revelation; both seeing God's activity in creation and new creation, both seeing a vision of an actual happening. I think this is a balanced position, taking 'both books' of God's revelation, (nature and the Bible)[249] seriously. Personally, I believe this world is old, not young. God has not only created it, being the first cause of everything but, through the ages, He has broken in at different times, to form and fill this 'privileged planet'.

This is Christianity's *origin story*. From the cosmic macro universe to micro cellular biology, this story is logical and coherent, with everything in its place and position. It is complex but accessible, it moves our emotions, and it satisfies our minds. It tells us who we are and where we are from. It gives enough information but not everything. It is cosmic but Earth-centred, poetic but actual, and gives us the proper foundation for understanding what it means to be human. It has the intuitive sense of being

---

[248] 'From the viewpoint of Earth, it started as "darkness was over the surface of the deep" (Genesis 1:2) because God "made the clouds its [the sea's] garment and wrapped it [the sea] in thick darkness" (Job 38:9, NIV). So, even though God had already created the "heavens" (Genesis 1:1), including our Sun and Moon, light did not yet reach Earth's surface. On creation day 1, when God said, "Let there be light" (Genesis 1:3, NIV), he transformed Earth's atmosphere from opaque to translucent. light is able to reach the planet surface. On Day 3 organic life comes, producing a great photsyntisis bringing an oxygen rich plant, in that he transformed Earth's atmosphere from translucent to at least occasionally be transparent. Later on creation day 4, when God said, "Let there be lights in the expanse of the sky ... They will serve as signs for seasons and for days and years" (Genesis 1:14). As he appointed them, Moses could see them.' This is a sum of the work of Dr Hugh Ross, *Improbable Planet*, https://reasons.org/explore/blogs/todays-new-reason-to-believe/hazy-early-Earth-more-affirmation-of-creation-day-4

[249] Psalm 19

true. Having said all that, the *how* is only part of the story; we must think seriously about the *why* of creation and, for that, we need another chapter.

CHAPTER 8

THE WHY, A LITTLE BIT FURTHER

But why, Mummy?

Every child under the sun

My daughters are at a stage when they ask fifty times more *why* questions than *how* questions. 'Why is the sun hot?', 'Why do we need to wear seatbelts?', 'Why are socks comfy?', 'Why are chips tasty?', 'Why do feet have toes?' Maybe this sounds familiar to you? We are naturally tuned this way: the *why* questions in life seem so much more relevant and intuitive to us. These are the questions that mean more to us because they are more concerned with our hearts than our heads. Genesis 1 goes beyond the history of things (the *how*), to the meaning of creation (the *why*), and it orders its material so we get the point. As I have said, the text hinges around *tohu* and *bohu* and organises the chapter into pairs of days. Days one and four, days two and five and days three and six, with verses 1–2 being an introduction and 2:1–3 a conclusion. If the text is structured this way, asking us to take these days as pairs and compare them, let's do that.

A word of warning: this is going to go way beyond deism but hopefully we will see that this text answers not only our 'grown up' *head* questions with the *how*, but our 'child-like' *heart* questions with the *why*. Genesis is the start of the story of the Bible, and it lays the foundation for the rest of God's revelation to us. At times I will naturally move forward in the story to see how the rest of the Bible interprets Genesis 1 and how it helps us understand these seeds of thought to give us a fuller understanding of the point that Genesis (and the Bible as a whole) is making. So please be patient with my jumps.

LIGHT, MEANING AND MORALITY

In days 1 and 4 the obvious thing underscored is light, and the fact that God is the source of this light. On day one, there is the initial light (whatever that is) and then on day 4 we have the appointment of the lights: the sun, moon, and stars. What does this mean?

Genesis 1 describes light, as we know and understand it, in terms of sun, moon and stars. In the New Testament Jesus refers to light,[250] using the physical sense of *how* we get our light[251] as a parable for deeper truths. Our light has its source outside this world, coming from the sun, 91–93 million miles away. Jesus applies this idea of light to show that certain things come from outside us, two things in particular: meaning[252] and morality.[253] These two things, like the light from our sun, cannot be produced 'in' us.

There is a deep seated 'feeling' among humans in general, including many atheists and agnostics, that there is something

---

[250] John 11:9-10
[251] David Gooding, *The God of New Beginnings*, 1975, p. 22
[252] John 8:10; 1 John 2:13-14
[253] Isaiah 5; John 3

beneath the surface of life and 'some *meaning* behind existence.'[254] We try to construct it ourselves through career, family and a hundred other transient things that inevitably fail. We crave a meaningful life, to have that purpose and direction, to see where we are going and to know the point of it all. Yet, Genesis teaches that meaning does not come from within us. Verse 2 speaks of a world in darkness. Imagine living in that world, never able to see where you are going, not knowing your surroundings and being unable to see the point of it all. Life would be meaningless and without direction. The New Testament apostle John applies this idea to say a person in darkness 'does not know where he is going because the darkness has blinded his eyes.'[255]

Meaning and purpose are basic building blocks of life and when people don't have them it causes tremendous fear and anxiety. One of the most haunting stories in the Bible is the story of Cain and Abel.[256] Cain chooses to live his own way, for himself, not acknowledging his Creator. He takes the gift given to him by God—being able to work the land—uses it on himself and then forgets God. Living for himself leads to jealousy towards his brother and eventually he kills him. Afterwards, God confronts him and, because of his actions, banishes him to a life of 'wandering'. Cain cries out, saying, 'My punishment is greater than I can bear.'[257] Genesis 1 is telling us that meaning and purpose come from the Creator. If we throw off our Creator, where does that leave us? Without Him we find ourselves aimlessly wandering in darkness 'not knowing where we are going'. I know people in my own city

---

[254] Paul Davies, *The Mind of God*, 1992, p. 16
[255] 1 John 2:11
[256] Genesis 4:1–16
[257] Genesis 4:13

who have thrown off God. They have taken His gifts and chosen to live for themselves, yet they are crying themselves to sleep, saying, 'This is greater than I can bear.' Why? Listen to this origin story: meaning has its source in the Creator.

When Jesus Christ came into this world, he said, 'I am the light of the world, he that follows me will have the light of life'[258]. In this, Jesus teaches that if you walk with Him and follow Him you will walk in the light and see what life is about. If there is a Creator, it follows that He will know what life is about. Just like light has a source, Genesis will teach us that God is the source of meaning. Imagine you were walking down the street with your friend and a beam of light appeared in front of you. If you asked, 'Where does that come from?' and your friend replied, 'It comes from nowhere,' you would say, 'Nonsense!' Just as light has a source, meaning has a source; not in this world, but in God Himself. If you want real, lasting meaning in your life; the kind of meaning that transcends circumstances and cannot be shaken by problems and suffering, it only comes from walking with God and letting Him show you what life is about.

The concept of *morality* is fascinating to think about, except when we are feeling guilty! Recently I read a brilliant short story called *The Most Dangerous Game* written by Richard Connell. It is the tale of a man, Rainsford, who is washed up on an island belonging to General Zarof. It turns out the General is a hunter of humans, and his island is his personal playground and reserve. When Rainsford confronts him, the General replies:

[258]   John 8:10

164

'I hunt the scum of the Earth—sailors from tramp ships—
lascars, blacks, Chinese, whites, mongrels—a thorough-
bred horse or hound is worth more than a score of them.'
'But they are men,' said Rainsford, hotly. 'Precisely,' said
the general. 'That is why I use them. It gives me pleasure.
They can reason, after a fashion. So, they are dangerous.'

We would all say that to murder a human, to hunt them for pleasure, is wrong. This is true of everyone's experience, regardless
of where or when they exist. They may go against that innate
impulse, wearing their conscience down until they could become
like General Zarof, but this is rare. We all usually have this moral
sense, the question is: why? Genesis 1, in the way it tells the creation story is putting its ancient finger on something core in this
universe: light. We have it naturally in the sun and cannot do
without it. Likewise, the rest of the Bible will teach that we have
light spiritually and cannot do without it. The Bible uses light as
a symbol for morality[259] and of God Himself[260] (the ultimate moral
authority). We humans believe it is wrong to murder, wrong to be
racist, wrong to lie, wrong to steal and wrong to invade another
country for your gain. But we also positively believe it is right to
treat your neighbour well, right to tell the truth or right to care
for the disadvantaged of society. There is a natural standard of
right and wrong that we live by. And if you read C. S. Lewis's *The
Abolition of Man* you will see clearly that this standard of positive benevolence runs right through every culture and religion.
It is as universal as light itself.

---

[259] Psalms 119:105, Matthew 5:14, James 1:17, John 3:19–21, Isaiah 60:19
[260] 1 John 1:5, Psalms 27:1, 104:2

This morality seems innate to us. Professor Paul Bloom, of Yale University, has for several years conducted studies in what he calls 'The Baby Lab'. Children from as young as five months old were shown a puppet show where one puppet is nice and the other puppet is mean. After a break, they are asked to choose which puppet they wanted to play with or to reward. By far, the majority choose the nice puppet. Some children even went as far as to strike the mean puppet as punishment.[261]

It is interesting that we favour the good but also have this keen sense of moral justice. The Guardian Newspaper recently ran a story about Mrs Andrews-Mann, who found her cat trapped in her bin one morning in quite some distress.[262] Living in London, where there are lots of CCTV cameras, she thought she might be able to get a glimpse of the culprit. She asked a neighbour and found the tape. To her shock, she saw a lady walk up, pet her cat, lift it and put it into the bin. Shocked, she put the footage on social media[263] to find out who the lady was, launching the justice of social media. The woman was discovered and quickly a campaign was launched against Mary Bale. Posters appeared calling for her death, she was described as 'evil' and a 'psycho' and there was even a Facebook page set up that demanded her sacking from her job as a customer services assistant with the Royal Bank of Scotland. Why did people care? What in us bothers so much about a cat that this kind of a storm would be kindled? We want justice because we are moral: we intuitively know what is right and wrong; that right should be praised and wrong punished.

---

[261] You can watch his lecture here: *https://www.youtube.com/watch?v=KKDOLIdbOtI*

[262] *https://www.theguardian.com/world/2010/aug/25/ mary-bale-lola-cat-wheelie-bin*

[263] You can watch the footage here: *https://www.youtube.com/ watch?v=NjlTaU3TUDY*

Genesis not only tells us that we are created, but that we are created in a certain way. We are made in the image of God, like Him, and He is good. We are made moral. There is a God behind this universe and the morality in humanity points to Him. We try to fight against it, but most of us know it is there. In telling how he come to Faith, A.N Wilson, a former atheist, noticed this:

> All my secular friends and me, all of us who didn't believe in God insisted that people care about justice, insisted that people not trample on the poor, insisted that people believe in human rights. If there is no God, there is absolutely no right for talking like that! We are here by accident, just animated pieces of meat, no purpose . . . . *just/unjust* that's just your opinion, yet you insist there really is right and wrong and justice and judgment. We were living like there was a God, because we know there is a God but won't admit it.[264]

This may be true, but where does morality come from? Genesis will tell us that like light, morality has a source, and that source is God Himself. I think we know this by intuition.

THE WORLD BEYOND

When we learn to look inside ourselves, we find that we have intrinsic desires and intuitive notions that we cannot easily shake. We desire relationships but when they are broken, for example by death, we have an instinctive desire for reconciliation, a longing

---

[264] Quoted Tim Keller, *The Reason for God*, 2008

to see those we have lost. I would dare to say it is almost a belief. Have you noticed that we have a desire to outlast our bodies? Not just to live forever here, but an innate belief that we will exist somewhere after this life. We have a desire to see justice done. Not just here and now, but even for those who have died, like Hitler or Stalin or the murderer in the Columbine massacre; we believe that they should see justice. Why do we have this instinct, or desire, or belief? It seems to me that 'desires are a guide to the possible.'[265]

At the moment I am trying to shift a few of the pounds I gained at Christmas, so I have a desire to eat. Imagine having the desire to eat but there being no food. I love reading about this universe but imagine having a desire for understanding and there was nothing called 'knowledge'. We do not generally desire things that are not there in the first place. C. S. Lewis formulates this really well when he says:

> Creatures are not born with desires unless satisfaction for those desires exists, a baby feels hunger, well, there is such a thing as food. A duckling wants to swim, well, there is such a thing as water. Man feels sexual desires, well, there is such a thing as sex. If I find in myself a desire which no experience in this world can satisfy, the most probable explanation is that I was made for another world.[266]

If we have natural desires that equate with something to fulfil them, what about our 'eternal' desires? The innate knowledge

[265] Todd Buras and Michael Cantrell, C. S. Lewis' Argument from Nostalgia in Two Dozen or so Arguments for God, 2018, p. 356
[266] ibid.

of God, the hope of reconciliation, the hope of justice for this universe, the hope of peace and goodness in this world. Do these desires have equal satisfaction? The Bible teaches that they do. We are made, says the preacher in Ecclesiastes, 'with eternity in our hearts . . .'[267] We are born with an innate knowledge of God, says Paul. We have a desire for the eternal. One of our chief desires is that there is another world; that this life is not all there is.

Days two and five will teach us this in parable form. You will notice the emphasis, on the seas (1:6–7) and the heavens (1:8). On Day three we will see the land made for mankind but here on this day there are two areas outside our own, the waters and the heavens. The chaotic realm below us and the region above us. They are separated and formed on day two, but then they are filled on day five with birds and sea creatures. Adding to the detail of this pair, day two is the only day that it omits the phrase 'it was good'. I find it interesting that the seas are associated with judgement as they are used to bring the flood in Genesis 5–9.

The rest of the Bible will teach that there are two other realms outside of the Earth; there is a 'heaven' where God is, and a 'hell', which is without God. You can see the picture painted in this creation story but notice the progression of thought. If day one teaches us there is morality, and that there is a God behind it who is utterly moral and good, then we stand accountable to Him. Then days two and five teach us of two places beyond our Earth: a heaven,[268] a place of goodness and relationship with God; and there is a hell,[269] there is a place of punishment. This is serious.

---

[267] Ecclesiastes 3:11

[268] Revelation 14:11, 20:10, 15; 21:8; Matthew 13:41–50; 25:46; Mark 9:43; John 3:16–18; 2 Thessalonians 1:9; 2 Peter 2:4; Jude 1:7

[269] Matthew 22:29–33; John 14:2–6; Revelation 4–5; 7:13–17; 21:4–8; 22:3–7

If days one and four are right, if God is this good and this moral, we are in serious trouble. C. S. Lewis further says:

> If there is absolute goodness it must hate most of what we do. This is a terrible fix we are in . . . if the universe is governed then we are making ourselves enemies to that goodness every day and are not in the least likely to do any better tomorrow and so our case is hopeless again. We cannot do without God; we cannot do with him. God is the only comfort; he is also the supreme terror: The thing we most need and the thing we most want to hide from. He is our only possible ally, and we have made ourselves His enemies. Some people talk as if meeting the gaze of absolute goodness would be fun. They need to think again.[270]

I think he is right. This is one of the things the creation story starts to teach us; that if there is a God, and we have been created by Him, then we are accountable to Him and 'we are without excuse.'[271] We live in God's world and it is based on His moral justice. We all, like A. N. Wilson, have that platonic vision of moral justice, that wrongs must be righted! The Bible says this will happen:

> He has fixed a day on which he will judge the world in righteousness by a man whom he has appointed; and of this he has given assurance to all by raising him from the dead.[272]

---

[270] C. S. Lewis, *Mere Christianity*, 1974
[271] Romans 1:20–23
[272] Acts 17:30–31

What will happen when God accounts for ALL the wrongs of this world? Not just the Hitlers and Stalins, but the average Joes too. The Bible teaches us that there is a heaven and an 'under the Earth' and that they are separated. This is the serious reality of being created by a good and just God.

My point is this: that innate 'desire' you have for justice, for another world, for reconciliation and for life after death, is right. You can know it is right, not just because days two and five hint at it, but because there is someone who has come from that other world. Jesus Christ has been raised out of death and God 'has given assurance to all by raising him from the dead'. Jesus has been raised and He will stand on that great day of justice as the judge of this world. That is a solemn thing. We want justice, but we don't want to be judged ourselves.

UPRIGHT ANIMALS

My wife was sitting at a crossroads one day and a lorry carrying pigs went past, obviously heading to the abattoir. An that moment she thought to herself, *How normal a sight this is in a farming community but how different it would be if that lorry was filled with people.* What if it was a train filled with people on the way to Auschwitz? Why are humans different? Why are people of more value? Days three and six bring us to human life. On day three God makes the land, the inorganic matter, and then He creates organic matter. Again, standing between the two is, 'and God said'. On day six, God creates animals and then humans. What stands between animal life and human life? 'And God said'. The emphasis is on relatedness and distinctness. Matter is related to organic life, but utterly different. We are related to animals, yet we are completely distinct.

God treats humanity completely differently from anything else. He speaks to humanity, blesses them, gives them a position and purpose, provides them with food and gives them 'dominion' to steward this world for Him. How we have failed in this, raping and pillaging this world, rather than cultivating and subduing it. Shame on us. God speaks about mankind as being uniquely made in the 'image of God'. The root word means 'to cut off', 'to chisel', like a statue—making an image, likeness, or resemblance. An image both 'is and is not' what it resembles. We are 'God-like', but we are not God. We are 'animal-like', but not animal. We are unique. Think about this uniqueness for a moment. No animal has our conscience and intellect, our language and relationships, our pursuit of the world and scientific endeavour, our love of beauty or our culture; we are exceptional. This creation of humanity is not an afterthought: the previous days lead up to, and climax in, day six. It seems that everything in this chapter is leading to the creation of humans. God creates (*bara*) this universe (1:1), he creates (*bara*) complex life (1:21), and then he creates (*bara*) humans (1:27). Here we have levels of life: matter, organic, animal, and human. Humanity is the pinnacle of God's creation. We are immensely valued by this God who has created us.

We need to see this and again follow the progression of thought. If God is moral (days one, four) and we stand in judgement (days two, five), we are in trouble, because we don't live up to this moral standard. That is not the end of the story. God loves humanity (days three, six). He created the first humans unique in this world, with dignity and value and for a relationship with Him. He loves us so much that when we went astray, He sent

His Son Jesus Christ. He willingly came to take our place, to die for our sins and bear our punishment. That is, just like the days of Noah, where God made a way for humanity to be protected from judgement by providing an ark. God has created a way for us to be forgiven of our moral failures and to live with Him. The Bible says, 'For God so loved the world that he gave his one and only Son, that whoever believes in him shall not perish but have eternal life.'[273] Humanity stands at the centre of God's love and His plans for this universe. We are unique amongst God's creation and have a value that we cannot explain without the phrase 'made in his image and likeness'.

REST, SATISFACTION AND WHAT WE ARE LOOKING FOR

The seventh day is a day of rest. Let's consider a few details from Genesis 2:1–3. There is something about this day that God uniquely marks out as through this day God will bless all areas of life, from the natural to the spiritual. God stops his creating work, hallows and blesses this day. He blesses for life, for rule and for holiness, for the natural, political and the sacred in ascending order.[274] Next, notice that God stops his working and rests. Why? It wasn't as if He was tired, or out-of-puff. No, like an artist setting down his brushes and tools, He stops to enjoy his creation. Don't miss that; he wanted to enjoy His creation. Also, notice that this day has no 'day and night' ending formula. It was supposed to last forever. This seventh day is special; it is hallowed. Throughout

---

[273] John 3:16
[274] Kass, *The Beginning of Wisdom*, 2006, p. 53

the Bible this Sabbath day is referred to in several ways: showing God's enjoyment of His creation; as a prototype for the nation of Israel;[275] as a day with no work; in the New Testament, as a parable for salvation;[276] and then by Jesus Himself to describe the rest and satisfaction[277] we need.

Let's take up Jesus' idea of rest and satisfaction. Have you noticed how much we crave satisfaction, contentment, and rest? Most people seem to be happy most of the time, on the outside at least. But are most people satisfied most of the time? That's a much deeper question. Happy, as I hear it used, means 'happy enough', 'fine' or 'grand'. To be *satisfied* is to be deeply content, to have a deep buoyant joy no matter our circumstances. Most of us are not content; we are like Bono when he sang, 'I still haven't found what I'm looking for.' It is not just the 'broken people' of the world that feel this way, the apparently 'together' people feel it as too! In the Bible there was a man called Solomon. He was the wealthiest, wisest, most womanizing man you could have imagined. He had it all, so to speak. He had everything people think brings contentment. Startlingly, he says, 'I hated my life . . . my heart began to despair over all my toilsome labour under the sun.'[278] Jonathan Haidt in his book, *The Happiness Hypothesis*, says:

> The author of Ecclesiastes wasn't just battling the fear of meaninglessness but, he was battling the disappointment of success . . . nothing brought satisfaction.[279]

[275] Exodus 20:5
[276] Hebrews 4:1–11
[277] Matthew 11:28–30
[278] Ecclesiastes 2:17, 20
[279] Jonathan Haidt, *The Happiness Hypothesis*, 2006

Whether we are broken or together, C. S. Lewis again intuitively said of us . . .

> Most people, if they really learn how to look into their own hearts, know that they do want, and want acutely, something that cannot be had in this world. There are all sorts of things in this world that offer to give it to you, but they never keep their promise. The longings which arise in us when we first fall in love, or first think of some foreign country, or first take up some subject that excites us. There is in us a longing which no marriage, no travel, no learning can really satisfy. I am not speaking of what would ordinarily be called unsuccessful marriages or trips and so on, I am speaking of the best possible ones. The spouse may be a good one, the scenery has been excellent, it has turned out to be a good job, but "it" has evaded us.[280]

As Lewis points out, we want something that nothing in this life can give us. Even the good cannot truly satisfy, '"it" has evaded us.' If we are broken, we are not satisfied, yet if we have everything, like Solomon, we are not still satisfied. Travel, material goods, sensual gratification, success, and status will give quick spikes of pleasure and then fade. We are looking for satisfaction that doesn't fade and contentment that truly fulfils! We 'still haven't found what we're looking for.'

Jesus said, 'Come unto me all you who are weary and heavy, and I will give you rest'[281]. The message of the Christian gospel is

---

[280] C. S. Lewis, *Mere Christianity*, 1974
[281] Matthew 11:28

that Jesus Christ was born into this world to go to a cross, where he took our place for all the times we have rebelled against this moral God. He can give forgiveness; He can give satisfaction and He can give rest for our souls. Some have given up on religion because they feel burdened by the rules that come with it. They think that by keeping the rules, they can earn salvation from God. That if we can earn a 70% pass rate, maybe the 30% of our sinning doesn't matter. True Christianity is not like that. It is not earning salvation and working to keep the rules. No! Jesus has come and has died, was buried and is risen, to bear our sin and failures. If we repent of our wrongs and trust in him, at that very moment we can know forgiveness. That brings rest for our souls. To continue to get to know this God, to truly worship Him, brings satisfaction and pleasure to our hearts. St Augustine knew this when he said:

> Oh Lord, you made us for yourself, and our hearts are restless until they find their rest in you . . . . rightly then is my hope fixed strongly on him and this will heal all the diseases of my soul.[282]

WHERE TO START?

Where do we start? Genesis says, 'In the beginning God . . . .' What a parable for life and beyond. Above anything else, this chapter brings us to God. He creates, says, sees, separates, names, makes, appoints, blesses, finishes, makes holy and rests. In fact, God is the subject of virtually every action verb. God names the 'day',

[282] St Augustine, *Confessions*, n.d.

'night', 'heaven', 'sea' and 'Earth',[283] which means He is over it all. Genesis is saying this God is wise and powerful. He creates a diverse Earth filled with lavish provision. He is good. God is the source of the universe, of meaning, of morality, of judgement, of forgiveness, of humanity and of rest.

What surprises me, but makes sense to my intuition, is that Genesis doesn't set out to prove God. There is no bottom-up approach or illustration to help us understand. It just begins with God. The Bible says He just is. He exists. He is. He is not an object we evaluate, judge or even try to defend. He is the Creator who has made us. This changes the whole dynamic. We bow to Him, not the other way around. Let God be God! Derek Kidner says that Genesis 1:

> Orientates us and reveals the true proportion. The scientific account of the universe, realistic and indispensable as it is, overwhelms us with statistics that reduce our apparent significance to vanishing point. Not the prologue. Through the apparent naivete of this Earth centred and history centred account God says to each generation, whether it is burdened with the weight of factual knowledge which our own possesses, or with the misleading fantasies of ancient religions, 'stand here, on this Earth and in this present, to get the meaning of the whole. See this world is my gift uncharged to you, with the sun, moon and stars as its lamps and timekeepers, and its creatures under your care. See the present age as the time to which my creative work was moving, and the unconscious

---

[283] Genesis 1:5, 8, 10

aeons before it and see where it is heading, ultimately to
a Sabbath with God himself.[284]

Do you see what this origin story does? It goes right for the
source of everything; God and Genesis speak right to our hearts.
You can't tell me meaning, morality, guilt, forgiveness and judgement, love and human significance, environmental stewardship
and satisfaction have nothing to do with the fabric of life. They
do. They are core. Can you see how significant this chapter is? It
just makes sense of things. There comes a point when we have
to call a spade a spade. Genesis rings true, does it not?

'Na baintear an t-ainm den bhlonag', says my calendar today: 'If
it's lard, call it lard'. If what in front of you looks, smells, feels, and
tastes like lard, it's going to be lard. And, if it looks, smells, and
reasons like God, it might be God: 'If it's the Lord, call it the LORD'.
If we want this meaning, an answer to morality, fear of judgment
answered, a true relationship with God Himself and rest for our
souls, it all starts with the God who was there in the beginning.

Time for an epilogue . . .

[284] Derek Kidner, *Genesis*, 2008

EPILOGUE

One of my favourite books is *The Lion, the Witch and the Wardrobe* by C. S. Lewis. You may remember that, in the story, a young girl called Lucy finds her way into a room with a special wardrobe that transports her into another world: Narnia. When she returns, her brothers, Peter and Edmund, and her sister, Susan, don't believe her. Even when Edmund follows Lucy and goes to Narnia himself, he still denies it exists, lying to Susan and Peter. Lucy is left hurt and angry, but she keeps maintaining that she did go to Narnia. Susan and Peter are disturbed by Lucy's insistence that she has visited another world beyond their own and they confront the Professor who owns the house.

> "Logic," said the Professor half to himself. "Why don't they teach logic at these schools? There are only three possibilities. Either your sister is telling lies, or she is mad, or she is telling the truth. You know that she doesn't tell lies and it is obvious that she is not mad. For the moment then unless any further evidence turns up, we must assume that she is telling the truth."[285]

---

[285] C.S Lewis, *The Lion, The Witch and the Wardrobe*, 1950, p. 47

Despite it being the logical option, they had totally written off the 'supernatural' prospect of another world. I think I see something similar today and I wonder what the Professor would say to our situation. I wonder would logic without rhetoric or presupposition look like when we see the evidence for *something out there*, laid out for us in this book? I think we would all agree there are really only a couple of options as to why how to logically interpret the data.

One is that it is a fluke: a fluke of all flukes; a chance start to all things; a chance fine-tuning; a chance privileged planet; a chance start of organic life and a chance development to complex life. Some say to me, 'It's not blind luck, it is chance and necessity.' I honestly don't know what the difference is even after reading several works about it. It is luck, fluke and chance; that's what you have and the odds for all this are practically impossible. But let's say it is true, that this universe came together, through a 'law like gravity', or through 'nothing', then that makes no sense of our intuition. For the logical outcome is that we have no objective morality, no real meaning, no great purpose and point to life, no life after ours, no final judgement when things are made right and no God. That is a leap that my logic, and I guess the Professor's too, finds hard to accept.

The other option, and I would argue the more sensible one, the one that has a better probability of being true, the one that makes sense of our intuition is that there is a mind behind this universe, is that there is Something or Someone out there. Looking at these four great clues (the first cause, the fine-tuned start, the privileged planet and the complex cell), together with why science works and our intuition on life, then setting them alongside revelation and personal experience leaves me convinced. The Apostle Paul once said:

For what can be known about God is plain **to them**, because God has shown it to **[in] them**[286]. For his invisible attributes, namely, his eternal power and divine nature, have been clearly perceived, ever since the creation of the world, in the things that have been made. So they are without excuse. For although they knew God, they did not honour him as God or give thanks to him, but they became futile in their thinking, and their foolish hearts were darkened.[287]

Notice the double emphasis that God has revealed himself *to us* with creation, then revealed *in us* writing on our hearts his existence.

It isn't left to humanity whether they deduce God or not. God has revealed it to them; he has given this demonstration by the very fact of creation and what can be seen in creation. Ah, yes, but more than that. He has manifested it in them ... God has put a consciousness of the Creator into the heart of every human being.[288]

When we look at the world around us it is the most natural thing to perceive something out there, to perceive God's 'eternal power and divine nature.' To look into our intuition, it seems that we have to unlearn that there is a God, to fight against that awe that naturally comes when we study nature. So don't fight it. This is

---

[286] Translation by David Gooding, *God's Power for Salvation*, https ://www.myrtlefieldhouse.com/sermons/God's-power-for-salvation
[287] Romans 1:19-23
[288] David Gooding, *God's Power for Salvation*, 2005, p. 23

the point of this book. That you might be stirred to see as many others have, the Creator.

This is my layman's view of the universe.

APPENDIX 1

GENESIS 1–2:4 (ESV)

1 In the beginning, God created the heavens and the earth. 2 The earth was without form and void, and darkness was over the face of the deep. And the Spirit of God was hovering over the face of the waters.

3 And God said, "Let there be light," and there was light. 4 And God saw that the light was good. And God separated the light from the darkness. 5 God called the light Day, and the darkness he called Night. And there was evening and there was morning, the first day.

6 And God said, "Let there be an expanse in the midst of the waters, and let it separate the waters from the waters." 7 And God made the expanse and separated the waters that were under the expanse from the waters that were above the expanse. And it was so. 8 And God called the expanse Heaven. And there was evening and there was morning, the second day.

9 And God said, "Let the waters under the heavens be gathered together into one place, and let the dry land appear." And it was so. 10 God called the dry land Earth, and the waters that were gathered together he called Seas. And God saw that it was good.

11 And God said, "Let the earth sprout vegetation, plants yielding seed, and fruit trees bearing fruit in which is their seed, each according to its kind, on the earth." And it was so. 12 The earth brought forth vegetation, plants yielding seed according to their

own kinds, and trees bearing fruit in which is their seed, each according to its kind. And God saw that it was good. 13 And there was evening and there was morning, the third day.

14 And God said, "Let there be lights in the expanse of the heavens to separate the day from the night. And let them be for signs and for seasons, and for days and years, 15 and let them be lights in the expanse of the heavens to give light upon the earth." And it was so. 16 And God made the two great lights—the greater light to rule the day and the lesser light to rule the night—and the stars. 17 And God set them in the expanse of the heavens to give light on the earth, 18 to rule over the day and over the night, and to separate the light from the darkness. And God saw that it was good. 19 And there was evening and there was morning, the fourth day.

20 And God said, "Let the waters swarm with swarms of living creatures, and let birds fly above the earth across the expanse of the heavens." 21 So God created the great sea creatures and every living creature that moves, with which the waters swarm, according to their kinds, and every winged bird according to its kind. And God saw that it was good. 22 And God blessed them, saying, "Be fruitful and multiply and fill the waters in the seas, and let birds multiply on the earth." 23 And there was evening and there was morning, the fifth day.

24 And God said, "Let the earth bring forth living creatures according to their kinds—livestock and creeping things and beasts of the earth according to their kinds." And it was so. 25 And God made the beasts of the earth according to their kinds and the livestock according to their kinds, and everything that creeps on the ground according to its kind. And God saw that it was good.

26 Then God said, "Let us make man in our image, after our likeness. And let them have dominion over the fish of the sea and

over the birds of the heavens and over the livestock and over all the earth and over every creeping thing that creeps on the earth."

27   So God created man in his own image,
      in the image of God he created him;
      male and female he created them.

28 And God blessed them. And God said to them, "Be fruitful and multiply and fill the earth and subdue it, and have dominion over the fish of the sea and over the birds of the heavens and over every living thing that moves on the earth." 29 And God said, "Behold, I have given you every plant yielding seed that is on the face of all the earth, and every tree with seed in its fruit. You shall have them for food. 30 And to every beast of the earth and to every bird of the heavens and to everything that creeps on the earth, everything that has the breath of life, I have given every green plant for food." And it was so. 31 And God saw everything that he had made, and behold, it was very good. And there was evening and there was morning, the sixth day.

2 Thus the heavens and the earth were finished, and all the host of them. 2 And on the seventh day God finished his work that he had done, and he rested on the seventh day from all his work that he had done. 3 So God blessed the seventh day and made it holy, because on it God rested from all his work that he had done in creation.

4   These are the generations of the heavens and the
     earth when they were created, in the day that the
     LORD God made the earth and the heavens.

BIBLIOGRAPHY

Alexander, Denis R. *Creation or Evolution: Do We Have to Choose?* Oxford, UK: Monarch Books, 2008.

Altar, Robert. *Genesis.* New York: W. W. Norton and Company, 1996.

Atkinson, David. *The Message of Genesis 1–11.* Nottingham, England: InterVarsity Press, 1990.

Attenborough, David. *A Life on Our Planet.* Penguin Random House UK, 2020.

Augustine, St. *Confessions. n.d.*

—. *The City of God.* London: Hazell, Watson and Viney Ltd, 1934.

Behe, Michael. *Darwin's Black Box.* New York: Simon and Schuster, 1996.

—. *The Edge of Evolution: The Search for the Limits of Darwinism.* New York : Free Press, 2007.

Berlinski, David. *The Deniable Darwin.* Discovery Institute, 2009.

—. *The Devil's Delusion, Atheism and its Scientific Pretensions.* New York: Basic Books, 2009.

Brierley, Justin. *Unbelievable, Why, after ten years of talking with Atheists, I'm Still a Christian.* London: SPCK, 2017.

Budziszewski, J. *What We Can't Not Know.* San Francisco: Ignatius Press, 2003.

Burnell, Jocelyn Bell. *A Quaker Astronomer Reflects, Can a Scientist also be Religous?* Quakers Australia, 2013.

Calvin, John. *Genesis.* London: Banner of Truth, 1965.

Carroll, Sean. *The Big Picture, On the Origins of Life, Meaning and the Universe Itself.* London: Oneworld Publications, 2020.

Carson, D.A. *The God who is there.* Grand Rapids: Baker Books, 2010.

Collins, C. John. *Genesis 1-4: A Linguistic, Literary, and Theological Commentary.* New Jersey: P&R Publishing, 2006.

Collins, Francis. *The Language of God.* London: Simon and Schuster, 2007.

Cox, Brian and Andrew Cohen. *Human Universe.* London: William Collins, 2015.

Cox, Brian and Jeff Forshaw. *Why does E=mc2?* Croydon: CPI Group UK, 2009.

Craig, William Lane. *On Guard for Students, A Thinker's Guide to the Christian Faith.* Colorado Springs: David. C. Cook, 2015.

—. *The Kalam Cosmological Argument.* Oregon: Wipf and Stock Publishers, 1979.

Darwin, Charles. *The Origin of Species.* Oxford, London: Oxford University Press, 1996.

Davies, Paul. *The Demon in the Machine.* Penguin Books, 2019.

—. *The Eerie Silence, Searching for Ourselves in the Universe.* Penguin Books, 2011.

—. *The Goldilocks Enigma, Why the Universe is Just Right for Life?* Penguin Books, 2007.

—. *The Mind of God, Science and the Search for Ultimate Meaning.* New York: Simon and Schuster, 1992.

—. *The Origin of Life.* Penguin Books, 2003.

Dawkins, Richard. *River out of Eden, A Darwinian View of Life.* London: Weidenfeld and Nicolson, 2015.

—. *The Blind Watchmaker.* Penguin Random House UK, 2016.

—. *The God Delusion.* Transworld Publications, 2006.

DeHaan, Richard W. *The Living God.* Grand Rapids, Michigan: Zondervan Publishing House, 1973.

Dennett, Daniel C. *Darwin's Dangerous Idea, Evolution and the Meaning of Life.* Penguin Group, 1995.

Denton, Michael. *Evolution: Still a theory in Crisis*. Seattle: Discovery Institute Press, 2016.

—. *The Miracle of the Cell*. Seattle: Discovery Institute Press, 2020.

Dickson, John. *A Doubter's Guide to Jesus*. Grand Rapids: Zondervan, 2018.

Dyson, Freeman. *Disturbing the Universe*. New York: Harper and Row Publishers, 1979.

—. *Infinite in All Directions*. New York: Harper and Row Publishers, 1988.

Edwards, Simon. *The Sanity of Belief: Why Faith Makes Sense*. London: SPCK, 2021.

Enns, Peter. *The Evolution of Adam*. Grand Rapids: Brazos Press, 2012.

Eveson, Philip. *The Book of Origins*. Darlington: Evangelical Press, 2003.

Flew, Antony. *There is a God: How the World's Most Notorious Atheist Changed His Mind*. Harper Collin, 2007.

Fruchtenbaum, Arnold. G. *Ariel's Bible Commentary, The Book of Genesis*. Ariel Ministries, 2009.

Glass, David H. *Atheism's New Clothes: Exploring and Exposing the Claims of the New Atheists*. Nottingham: Apollos, 2012.

Goenka, Lakhi N. *Does the Atom have A Designer?* eThermal, LLC, 2016.

Gooding, David and John Lennox. *Being Truly Human, The Limits of our Worth, Power, Freedom and Destiny*. Belfast: Myrtlefield Trust, 2018.

Gordon, Timothy. *The Cosmological Argument for the Existence of God*. n.d.

Gould, Stephen Jay. *Wonderful Life: The Burgess Shale and the Nature of History*. London: Vintage, 2000.

Gray, John. *Straw Dogs*. London: Granta Books, 2003.

—. *Seven Types of Atheism*. Milton Keynes: Penguin Random House UK, 2018.

Green, Lucie. *15 Million Degrees, A Journey to the Centre of the Sun*. Penguin Books, 2017.

Hamilton, Victor P. *The Book of Genesis: Chapters 1–17*. Michigan: William B. Eerdmans Publishing Co., 1990.

Harari, Yuval Noah. *Sapiens; A Brief History of Humankind.* London: Penguin Random House UK, 2011.

Harber, Frank. *Prove it: Examing the Evidence of God's Existence.* Tennessee: Engedi Publishing, 2003.

Hawking, Stephen. *Brief Answers to the Big Questions.* Space Time Publications, 2018.

Henry, Matthew. *Matthew Henry's Commentary on the Whole Bible: Complete and Unabride in One Volume.* Peabody and Hendrickson, 1996.

Hess, Richard S. *God and Origins: Interpreting the Early Chapters of Genesis.* Berry, R. J. and T. A. Nobel.

—. *Darwin, Creation and the Fall.* Nottingham, England: Inter-Varsity Press, 2009. 90-92.

Hitchens, Christopher. *God is Not Great.* Atlantic Books, 2008.

Hitchens, Peter. *The Rage Against God: How Atheism Led Me to God.* Grand Rapids: Zondervan, 2010.

Hoffmeier, James, Gordon Wenham and Kenton Sparks. *Genesis: History, Fiction, or Neither?* Michigan: Zondervan, 2015.

Holt, Jim. *Why does the World Exist?* London: Profile Books, 2012.

Howatson, M.C. *The Oxford Companion to Classical Literature (2nd ed.).* Oxford: Oxford University Press, 1997.

Hughes, R. Kent. *Genesis.* Wheaton, Illinois: Crossway Books, 2004.

Kaku, Michio. *The God Equation: The Quest for a Theory of Everything.* Dublin: Penguin Random House UK, 2021.

Kampouurakis, Kostas. *Understanding Genes.* Cambridge: Cambridge University Press, 2022.

Kass, Leon. *The Beginning of Wisdom.* Chicago: University of Chicago Press, 2006.

Keller, Timothy. *Making Sense of God.* London: Hodder and Stoughton, 2018.

—. *The Reason for God, Belief in an Age of Scepticism.* London: Hodder and Stoughton, 2008.

Kidner, Derek. *Genesis*. England: IVP, 2008.

Krauss, Lawrence. *A Universe from Nothing, Why there is Something Rather than Nothing*. London: Simon and Schuster, 2012.

—. *The Greatest Story Ever Told . . . So Far, why are we here?* Simon and Schuster, 2018.

Lane, William. *The New International Commentary on the New Testament, The Gospel according to Mark*. Grand Rapids, Michigan: William B. Eerdmans Publishing Company, 1974.

Latham, Anthony. *The Naked Emperor: Darwinism Exposed*. Cambridge: Janus Publishing Co., 2005.

Leidner, Gordon. *Of God and Dice*. 2012.

Lennox, John C. *Can Science Explain Everything?* Good Book Company, 2019.

—. *God and Stephen Hawking, Whose Design is it Anyway?* Lion Hudson, 2010.

—. *God's Undertaker: Has Science buried God?* Oxford, London: Lion Hudson PLC, 2009.

—. *Seven Days that Divide the World: The Beginnings According to Genesis and Science*. Grand Rapids, Michigan, USA: Zondervan, 2011.

Lewis, C. S. *God in the Dock*. Grand Rapids: Wm. B. Eerdmans Publishing Co., 197-.

—. *Mere Christianity*, 1942

—. *Miracles*. New York: Harper Collins, 1974.

—. *The Chronicles of Narnia, The Lion, the Witch and the Wardrobe*. London: Harper Collins, 1950.

Lewis, Geraint F., and Barnes, Luke A. *A Fortunate Universe, Life in a Finely Tuned Cosmos*. Cambridge: Cambridge University Press, 2020.

Lightman, Alan. *The Accidental Universe*. New York: Pantheon Books, 2013.

MacArthur, John. *The Battle for the Beginning*. Nelson Books, 2001.

Mackintosh, C. H. *Notes on the Book of Genesis*. Warwick Lane, London: Loizeaux Bros, 1857.

McGrath, Alister. *Mere Apologetics. Grand Rapids*: Baker Books, 2012.

—. *The Great Mystery, Science, God and the Human Quest for Meaning*. London: Hodder and Stoughton, 2017.

McGrath, Alister. *Mere Apologetics. Grand Rapids*: Baker Books, 2012.

—. *The Great Mystery, Science, God and the Human Quest for Meaning*. London: Hodder and Stoughton, 2017.

McLaughlin, Rebecca. *Confronting Christianity*. Crossway, 2019.

Metaxas, Eric. *Is Atheism Dead?* Washington D.C.: Salem Books, 2021.

Meyer, Stephen C. *Return of the God Hypothesis*. New York: Harper Collins, 2021.

—. *Signature in the Cell*. New York: Harper Collins, 2009.

Mitton, Simon. *Fred Hoyle: A Life in Science*. London: Aurum Press Ltd, 2005.

Nagel, Thomas. *Mind and Cosmos*. Oxford: Oxford University Press, 2012.

Nevin, Norman C. *Should Christians Embrace Evolution?* Nottingham: IVP, 2009.

Berry, R. J. and Noble, T. A. *Darwin, Creation and the Fall*. London: IVP, 2009.

Nurse, Paul. *What is Life?: Understand Biology in Five Steps*. Oxford: David Fickling Books, 2020.

Pageau, Matthew. *The Language of Creation: Cosmic Symbolism in Genesis*. 2018.

Parker, Andrew. *The Genesis Enigma*. London: Black Swan, 2010.

Plantinga, Alvin. *Knowledge and Christian Belief. Grand Rapids*: Eerdmens Publishing, 2015.

—. *Warranted Christian Belief*. New York: Oxford University Press, 2000.

—. *Where the Conflict Really Lies: Science, Religion & Naturalism*. Oxford: Oxford University Press, 2011.

Polkinghorne, John C. *Science and Providence, God's Interaction with the World*. Templeton Foundation Press, 2005.

Pfundner, Michael and Ernest Lucus. *Think God, Think Science*. Colorado Springs: Paternoster, 2008.

BIBLIOGRAPHY

Rees, Martin. *Just Six Numbers: The Deep Forces that Shape the Universe.* London: Orion Books Ltd, 1999.

—. *Our Cosmic Habitat.* Oxfordshire: Princeton University Press, 2017.

Reich, David. *Who We Are and How We Got Here.* Oxford: Oxford University Press, 2019.

Richards, Jay and Gonzalez, Guillermo. *The Privileged Planet.* Washington: Regnery Publishing, 2020.

Ross, Hugh. *Improbable Planet; How Earth became Humanitys Home.* Grand Rapids: Baker Books, 2017.

—. *Why the Universe is the Way it is.* Grand Rapids: Baker Books, 2008.

Rovelli, Carlo. *Seven Brief Lessons on Physics.* Penguin Random House UK, 2015.

Sacks, Jonathan. *The Great Partnership, God, Science and the Search for Meaning.* London: Hodder and Stoughton, 2012.

Sagan, Carl. *The Dragons of Eden.* Random House Publishing, 1977.

Schaeffer, Francis. *Genesis in Space and Time.* IVP, 1972.

—. *The God Who is There.* Hodder and Stoughton, 1970.

Schrodinger, Erwin. *What is Life?* Cambridge University Press, 2018.

Stannard, Russell. *Science and Belief: The Big Issues.* Lion Hudson PLC, 2012.

Stenger, Victor. *The Comprehensible Cosmos.* New York: Prometheus Books, 2006.

Stigers, Harold. *A Commentary On Genesis.* Michigan: Zondervan Publishing House, 1976.

Stott, John. *Basic Christianity.* Nottingham: InterVarsity Press, 2008.

—. *The Bible Speaks Today, The Message of Romans.* Nottingham: IVP, 1994.

Strobel, Lee. *The Case for a Creator.* Michigan: Zondervan, 2004.

Swinburne, Richard. *Is there a God?* Oxford: Oxford University Press, 1996.

Tegmark, Max. *Our Mathematical Universe: My Quest for the Ultimate Nature of Reality.* Penguin Books, 2015.

Tinker, Melvin. *That Hideous Strength: How the West was Lost.* EP Books, 2018.

Tonelli, Guido. *Genesis, The Story of How Everything Began.* London: Profile Books, 2021.

Turek, Frank. *Stealing from God: Why Atheists need God to Make their Case.* Nav Press, 2014.

Veale, Graham. *New Atheism, A Survival Guide.* Christian Focus, 2013.

Walton, John H. *The Lost World of Genesis One.* IVP, 2009.

Ward, Keith. *God, Chance and Necessity.* Oxford: Oneworld Publications, 2009.

—. *The Evidence for God, The Case for the Existance of the Spiritual Dimension.* London: Darton, Longman and Todd Ltd, 2014.

—. *Why the most Certainly Is a God.* Oxford: Lion Hudson PLC, 2008.

Walls, Jerry L., and Dougherty, Trent. eds. *Two Dozen (or so) Arguments for God: The Plantinga Project.* New York: Oxford University Press, 2018.

Walton, John H. *The Lost World of Genesis One: Ancient Cosmology and the Origins Debate.* Madison, USA: InterVarsity Press, 2009.

Wenham, Gordon J. *Rethinking Genesis 1–11; The Didsbury Lectures.* Oregon: Cascade Books, 2013.

—. *Word Biblical Commentary, Vol 1: Genesis 1–15.* Dallas: Thomas Nelson, 1987.

Wilkinson, David. *The Message of Creation.* Nottingham: Inter-Varsity Press, 2002.

Williams, Peter S. *A Faithful Guide to Philosophy.* Milton Keynes: Paternoster, 2013.

—. *A Sceptic's Guide to Atheism.* London: Paternoster, 2009.

—. *I wish I could Believe in Meaning.* Hampshire: Damaris Publishing, 2004.

ENDORSEMENTS

Is science in conflict with belief in God? In this highly readable book, John Hewitt investigates the big questions about the nature of the universe and our place within it to argue that there is no such conflict. Along the way, he explores fascinating scientific issues relating to the origin of the universe, fine-tuning of physical constants, unique features of Earth that make life possible and the complexity of life itself. Sceptics may doubt that scientific findings and the very nature of science point to God, but I encourage them to read this book with an open mind to see if there might just be something out there.

— Dr David Glass: Senior Lecturer in Computer Science at Ulster University and author of *Atheism's New Clothes* (Apollos).

John Hewitt has done us the great service of distilling the complexities of recent scientific discoveries to show how they fit within a Christian worldview. As he unpacks their implications, both believers and sceptics will have to admit there are real questions to be answered, but also that there are answers to honest questions; and both are important for us if we are going to understand the truth about our universe and our place in it.

— Dr Joshua Fitzhugh, Executive Director, The Myrtlefield Trust / Myrtlefield House

John Hewitt has written a well-researched and witty introductory text, offering readers an informed overview of how contemporary science repeatedly raises questions to which the God hypothesis offers a reasonable answer."

John Hewitt has done an amazing job, as a scientific layman, in reading and understanding more sophisticated books about science and faith in God than even many scientists ever have, I guess! Using a fresh breeze of humour, he explains in a captivating way the basic arguments, full of catchy/memorable illustrations, how the science of our universe not only goes along well with believe in a personal God, but even provides good evidence that there is someone special out there. This book is an easy to read primer for everyone, offering further solid material in the bibliography to even dig deeper wherever you want to dig ...

ND - #0045 - 260723 - C0 - 198/129/11 - PB - 9781787989504 - Gloss Lamination